DREAM TO Destiny

A Proven Guide to
Navigating Life's Biggest Tests
and Unlocking Your
God-Given Purpose

ROBERT MORRIS

GATEWAY®
PUBLISHING

BETHANYHOUSE
a division of Baker Publishing Group
Minneapolis, Minnesota

GATEWAY®
PUBLISHING

We hope you hear from the Holy Spirit and receive God's richest blessings from this book by Gateway Publishing®. Our purpose is to carry out the mission and vision of Gateway Church through print and digital resources to equip leaders, disciple believers, and advance God's kingdom. For more information on other resources from Gateway Publishing, visit GatewayPublishing.com.

Gateway Publishing
500 S Nolen, Suite 300
Southlake, TX 76092
GatewayPublishing.com

Cover illustration by Joshua Noom.

Printed in the United States of America.
23 24 25 26 27—5 4 3 2 1

TABLE OF CONTENTS

Introduction

Everyone loves a good story. Most of us were brought up listening to stories our parents, grandparents, and teachers told us or read to us. We pretended and acted out stories, alone or with friends. Even as adults we listen to stories on the radio, podcasts, or records. We read books with stories and go to the movies to watch stories. We even experience stories in our dreams.

So, what makes a good story? A good plot. Interesting characters— heroes and villains. Exciting action. Drama and intrigue. Surprise twists. And a happy ending.

The biblical story of Joseph in *Dream to Destiny* has all of these—and more!

You see, God is the *Master Storyteller*, and the Bible is His collection of stories of real events recorded and retold by people over thousands of years. Some stories are as old as time, but God's stories are even *older than time*! God had His plans for us before the creation of the world (see Ephesians 1:4–6). And we are all part of His much greater story!

Many Bible stories are well-known in popular culture, even to the unchurched: Adam and Eve in the Garden of Eden. Noah and the flood. Moses and the Ten Commandments. David and Goliath. Jesus on the cross. If you were brought up going to church, I'm sure you're familiar with these and many others.

The story of Joseph has also gained a special place in popular culture. The well-known musical *Joseph and the Amazing Technicolor Dreamcoat* was first performed in the West End of London in 1973 and on Broadway in 1982 (and later made into a movie). It, too, was popular with children: the first version was originally written as a short oratorio/cantata for children in 1968.[1] It was the first notable collaboration of the now legendary composer Andrew Lloyd Webber and lyricist Tim Rice. You might say it was the beginning of their musical journey.

Joseph's story was definitely a journey—a decades-long journey toward his destiny. *And it's a journey every one of us must also take.*

This study guide will lead you through each chapter of *Dream to Destiny* and help you navigate the ten character-building tests that Joseph faced throughout his journey, because all of us will face these same tests. Some tests are more difficult than others. Some take longer than others. Some must be faced more often than others. Regardless, we will all face these tests on the road to our destinies. This study guide will tie the eternal principles of these tests together using Scripture, examples of other Bible characters, and modern-day, real-life stories and examples. It will challenge you to have a deeper understanding of these truths and help you apply them in your everyday life.

You can use this study guide for individual study or for discussion in a family or small group setting. And just as the apostle Paul spoke to his beloved disciple, Timothy, I urge you to "do your best to present yourself to God as one approved, a worker who does not need to be ashamed and who correctly handles the word of truth" (2 Timothy 2:15 NIV). May this study guide help God's Word come alive in a new way and give you answers to many of the questions you may have about the journey to your destiny.

My prayer, as Paul writes in Romans 12:2, is that you "do not be conformed to this world, but be transformed by the renewing of your mind, that you may prove what is that good and acceptable and perfect will of God," and that your doing so will help enable God's will to be done "on earth as it is in heaven" (Matthew 6:10).

God's dream for you is bigger than you can imagine! And it is through these character-building tests that He prepares you to reach your unique destiny.

Remember, God is the author of *your* story, and He will speak to you just as He spoke to Joseph. He will speak to you in dreams. He will speak to you through prophets. He will speak to you through His Word. He will speak to you through the Holy Spirit. He may even speak to you directly.

Your job is simply to hear, believe, and obey. If you follow God's simple plan and instructions, then you, like Joseph, can follow your God-given dream and fulfill your destiny.

CHAPTER ONE

The Pride Test

An experience in my mid-twenties was my first major encounter with the Pride Test. I got saved at the age of nineteen, and just ten months later, I started working for James Robison, an evangelist preaching citywide evangelistic crusades. I traveled with him and spoke at junior and senior high school assemblies. I had not even been a Christian for a year when I began to travel and preach the gospel. Heady stuff for someone so young (and even younger in the Lord!).

Though I started out speaking at public schools, soon I was preaching to large crowds at crusades. James was even gracious enough to give me a title: associate evangelist.

It seemed to me that the favor of God was on everything I touched. What a destiny lay before me! What could stop me now?

By the time I was twenty-five, I had become accustomed to hearing people tell me how gifted I was—and I began to expect it. I really believed it when people said I was gifted and could do anything. I believed *I was really successful!*

In retrospect, it's clear that an enemy called pride had crept into my life, taking up residence in my heart and mind.

Have you ever been promoted to a role or position that seemed to be beyond what might have expected because of your age or lack of experience? How did it feel? Did it cause any problems for you? (You could also draw upon an example of someone you know.)

_____

_____

_____

_____

What did people praise you for when you received that role or promotion?

_____

_____

_____

_____

How did you react to the praise you received? Where do you think those thoughts originated?

_____

_____

_____

_____

I recognized the pride in my life, but I didn't know what to do about it. So, I began to pray and ask God for help. I prayed, "God, I know I have pride. I know my insecurity makes me vulnerable to it. I need to be free of this, but I don't know what to do!" I asked the Lord, "What can I do about this? Is there anything I can do to deal with the pride in my life?"

The Lord told me to step out of ministry and look for a regular job. I wasn't thrilled about what He said, but I was obedient and did it.

Has the Lord ever told you to do something you didn't want to do? Did you choose to be obedient?

_____

_____

_____

_____

Have you ever stepped away from a job or situation you thought was unproductive or even damaging to your life? Explain.

_____

_____

_____

_____

What did you learn from being obedient and stepping away from that job or situation?

_____

_____

_____

_____

Have you ever had a strong sense God was leading you to a major life change? If so, how did you react to His leading?

_____

_____

_____

_____

Eventually, I felt I had made strides toward humility and returned to James Robinson's ministry as a supervisor at their prayer center— clearly a lower position than associate evangelist. And I still had some work to do about pride, as evidenced that morning when Terry Redmon, James Robison's son-in-law, heard me on the phone talking to the woman who had called for prayer and recognized my voice. I made a prideful statement on the phone, and afterward Terry called me out on it.

Have you ever made a prideful statement similar to the one I made? What was the result? Why do you think you said it?

_____

_____

_____

_____

How did I react to Terry's evaluation of my behavior?

_____

_____

_____

_____

What was the fundamental principle I missed when suggesting the woman on the phone might be blessed by knowing I was an "associate evangelist"?

_____

_____

_____

_____

What was the great lesson about destiny and responsibility this incident caused me to realize?

_____

_____

_____

_____

Seasons of Testing

For us to fulfill our God-given dreams, we must have God's character. That's why He allows us to go through tests on our way from the dream to the destiny.

Is there a dream God has put in your heart?

_____

_____

_____

_____

I received a God-given dream at a young age. And thousands of years ago, Joseph also received a monumental dream from God. He then went through a long season of testing to get to the destiny that dream predicted. His faithfulness in walking through and passing ten distinct character tests helped him step into that destiny, and the fulfillment of God's dream was a great blessing not only to Joseph but to millions of people and an entire nation. We must also walk through and pass those same tests to fulfill our destiny.

According to the book, how many chances will we get to pass these tests? Who does the grading, and what does a passing grade enable us to do?

_____

_____

_____

_____

The Pride Test: Revealing the Pride Within

Genesis 37 describes how Joseph first received his dream from God and how he handled it when the dream came.

> Joseph, being seventeen years old, was feeding the flock with his brothers. And the lad was with the sons of Bilhah and the sons of Zilpah, his father's wives; and Joseph brought a bad report of them to his father.
>
> Now Israel loved Joseph more than all his children, because he was the son of his old age. Also he made him a tunic of many colors. But when his brothers saw that their father loved him more than all his brothers, they hated him and could not speak peaceably to him.
>
> Now Joseph had a dream, and he told it to his brothers; and they hated him even more. So he said to them, "Please hear this dream which I have dreamed: There we were, binding sheaves in the field. Then behold, my sheaf arose and also stood upright; and indeed your sheaves stood all around and bowed down to my sheaf."

And his brothers said to him, "Shall you indeed reign over us? Or shall you indeed have dominion over us?" So they hated him even more for his dreams and for his words.

Then he dreamed still another dream and told it to his brothers, and said, "Look, I have dreamed another dream. And this time, the sun, the moon, and the eleven stars bowed down to me."

So he told it to his father and his brothers; and his father rebuked him and said to him, "What is this dream that you have dreamed? Shall your mother and I and your brothers indeed come to bow down to the earth before you?" And his brothers envied him, but his father kept the matter in mind. (Genesis 37:2–11)

Why do you think Joseph's brothers hated him?

_____

_____

_____

_____

Have you ever experienced a situation where you were excited about a dream or goal and had to deal with other people's negative feelings or opinions about it? If so, elaborate.

_____

_____

_____

_____

What are the similarities between Joseph's two dreams? The differences?

_____

_____

_____

_____

What do you think it means that Joseph's father "kept the matter in mind"?

_____

_____

_____

_____

How long would it be between the time of Joseph's dreams and when he began to see them fulfilled? What was the fundamental reason for the tests Joseph would have to face? Explain.

_____

_____

_____

_____

Notice that Joseph's dreams were not his destiny. His purpose was not to rule over his family. What destiny was God preparing for Joseph?

_____

_____

_____

_____

According to the book, there were two main reasons God did not give Joseph dreams that showed his ultimate purpose or destiny.

What was the first reason God did not show Joseph the ultimate purpose of his dreams? Explain.

_____

_____

_____

_____

What was the second reason God did not show Joseph the ultimate purpose of his dreams? Explain.

_____

_____

_____

_____

God knew Joseph would never step into his destiny until the sin of pride in his heart had been exposed and dealt with. It was the catalyst for his character change. In the same way, God knows exactly the kind of dream He needs to give you to get you started.

God also provides opportunities for us to take a test repeatedly until we pass. God is a God of second chances, as we see in many examples throughout the Bible.

Abraham and Sarah: Read Genesis 12. What was God's promise and plan for their destiny?

_____

_____

_____

_____

What did Abraham do in Genesis 12:10–13?

_____

_____

_____

_____

Read Genesis 20:1–3. Had Abraham learned his lesson? What did Abraham do again? What seems to be Abraham's main sin problem (see verse 2)? Explain.

_____

_____

_____

_____

Read Genesis 16. What did Abraham fail to do in this chapter?

_____

_____

_____

_____

God gave this couple many chances over a long period of time before they finally fulfilled God's plan for them.

David: Read 2 Samuel 11–12. How did this show God's willingness to give second chances?

_____

_____

_____

_____

If you are stuck on the path to your destiny, what are some areas of your character you need to let God change and improve?

_____

_____

_____

_____

How does Zechariah 13:9 apply to this?

_____

_____

_____

_____

Dealing with Pride

Why is pride often the first and most frequent test we face?

_____

_____

_____

What examples are given in the text? Can you think of some others?

_____

_____

_____

_____

The Problem Is Your Tongue

According to Genesis 37:8, what is the secondary reason Joseph's brothers hated him?

_____

_____

_____

_____

Where do you fall on the "humble to bragging" spectrum of talking about yourself? Are you prone to self-promotion? Explain and give an example.

_____

_____

_____

_____

How do you feel or respond when you hear someone engage in self-promotion or boasting?

_____

_____

_____

_____

Explain the difference between giving a testimony or sharing about the work God has done in your life versus bragging about how God has moved through you. What is the main difference?

_____

_____

_____

_____

What happens when we take the glory meant for God and bask in it ourselves?

_____

_____

_____

_____

Respond to this statement: "To get control of our bragging, some of us simply need to stop talking for a while."

_____

_____

_____

_____

What did I ask Debbie to do to help me in this area? Have you ever asked someone to do something similar to help you? Explain.

_____

_____

_____

_____

The *Real* Problem Is in Your Heart

Read Matthew 12:34 and Matthew 15:18. In what way is bragging more of a heart problem than a mouth problem?

_____

_____

_____

_____

The Root of Pride

What are three words that describe the root of pride?

_____

_____

_____

Describe a time when you (or someone you know well) exhibited a behavior brought out by one or more of these feelings.

_____

_____

_____

_____

After my prideful comment about the success of my ministry during the Shady Grove Church reunion honoring Pastor Olen Griffing and his wife, what did the Lord remind me was the underlying issue?

_____

_____

_____

_____

If pride is in your heart, then insecurity, inferiority, or inadequacy is in your soul (your mind, will, and emotions). Essentially, your thoughts, decisions, and feelings are the building blocks of your soul, and when insecurity, inferiority, or inadequacy become the driving force behind what you think, do, and feel, pride has a chance to infiltrate your heart.

What lies behind feelings of insecurity, inferiority, or inadequacy? Explain.

_____

_____

_____

_____

Our accomplishments, no matter how impressive, are not what make us valuable. Even our dreams from God, as wonderful and awe-inspiring as they might be, are not *who* we are.

Second Samuel 24:1–17 tells the story about a time David had pride in his heart, and the consequences were fatal. Against the advice of Joab, his commander of the army, David took a census of Israel to enlarge the army. This was a sign of pride, because David was insecure and wanted a larger fighting force despite the protection and success God had always provided him.

David quickly recognized and repented of his sin, but not before seventy thousand Israelites died from a plague. The toll would have been even higher had God not withheld His hand from Jerusalem at the last minute.

David's pride was truly deadly.

According to the book, where do we find our true identity? What happens when we become comfortable and secure in that identity?

_____

_____

_____

_____

How secure do you feel in your true identity in Christ?

_____

_____

_____

_____

What was the first thing Satan did to tempt Jesus when He was in the wilderness (see Matthew 4:1–11)?

_____

_____

_____

How did Jesus respond to this temptation?

_____

_____

_____

_____

When we are tempted with feelings of insecurity, inferiority, or inadequacy, we must go back to what God our Father has said about us and rest in that truth.

Your Identity in Christ

It's vital to understand that the ultimate key to your victory over pride is knowing who you are in Christ.

Jesus knew who He was in His relationship with the Father, so He didn't have to prove anything about Himself. In the same way, you must come to the place where your identity is in Christ and in your relationship *with* Him—not in what you do *for* Him. If your identity is in what you do or the name you've built for yourself, then you are failing the Pride Test.

What are the two powerful weapons you can use to root out insecurity, inferiority, and inadequacy and prevent pride from thriving in your life? Explain each.

1. _____

   _____

2. _____

   _____

When we pass the Pride Test, we can be a "nobody" or do "nothing" and still be confident, content, and at peace because the greatest joy in life comes from knowing God.

If God continues to use us to do grand things, that's great! And if He uses someone else to a greater degree, that's wonderful, too, because being a follower of Christ is not about proving what we can do for God—*it's about receiving all He has already done for us.* It's about knowing Him and allowing Him to work in our lives, helping us fulfill the roles He has given us.

Read Matthew 5:19 and 19:27–30. What do these passages teach about being least or greatest?

_____

_____

_____

_____

Humble Yourself

The Bible never tells us to pray for humility. It simply tells us to humble ourselves. First Peter 5:6 says, "Therefore *humble yourselves* under the mighty hand of God, that He may exalt you in due time" (emphasis added). So how do you humble yourself? I have found an easy method: spend time with God every day.

Why is it easier to be humble when you spend time in the presence of God every day? Explain.

_____

_____

_____

_____

What are some things you can do to experience the Lord's presence? Explain.

_____

_____

_____

_____

How important is accountability to avoiding prideful behavior? Do you have someone in your life who can provide feedback and hold you accountable?

_____

_____

_____

_____

As you spend time with God, He will show you who you really are in Him. He will help you understand the security you have as His son or daughter. This is how you stay humble and pass the Pride Test. Then you can move forward on the path to discovering the wondrous destiny He has prepared for you.

For Further Reflection

Proverbs 8:13

Proverbs 16:5

1 John 2:16

Psalm 10:4

1 Timothy 3:6

Key Quotes

For us to fulfill our God-given dreams, we must have God's character.

God knows exactly the kind of dream He needs to give you to get you started.

Our accomplishments, no matter how impressive, are not what make us valuable. Even our dreams from God, as wonderful and awe-inspiring as they might be, are not who we are.

When we are tempted with feelings of insecurity, inferiority, or inadequacy, we must go back to what God our Father has said about us and rest in that truth.

As you spend time with God, He will show you who you really are in Him.

CHAPTER TWO

The Pit Test

The Pit Test: Finding Your Way Out

Like it or not, all of us will go through times when we feel as if we are in a pit. We may not be sure how we got there and even less sure how to get ourselves out. But one thing is certain: we won't move into our destiny unless we get out of the pit!

Joseph didn't just *feel* like he was in a pit; he was literally in one! He had just received those glorious dreams from God, and the future seemed bright and wonderful. Then suddenly he was stuck in a pit (see Genesis 37:24), and it began to seem like his dreams of honor and authority were just some cruel joke.

What caused Joseph to end up in the pit? What lessons would he have to learn before he could get out? Like Joseph, it's important for us to understand the lessons of the Pit Test, so we can pass it and move on.

Let's consider his story in Genesis 37:12–24.

Then his brothers went to feed their father's flock in Shechem. And Israel said to Joseph, "Are not your brothers feeding the flock in Shechem? Come, I will send you to them."

So he said to him, "Here I am."

Then he said to him, "Please go and see if it is well with your brothers and well with the flocks, and bring back word to me." So he sent him out of the Valley of Hebron, and he went to Shechem.

Now a certain man found him, and there he was, wandering in the field. And the man asked him, saying, "What are you seeking?"

So he said, "I am seeking my brothers. Please tell me where they are feeding their flocks."

And the man said, "They have departed from here, for I heard them say, 'Let us go to Dothan.'" So Joseph went after his brothers and found them in Dothan.

Now when they saw him afar off, even before he came near them, they conspired against him to kill him. Then they said to one another, "Look, this dreamer is coming! Come therefore, let us now kill him and cast him into some pit; and we shall say, 'Some wild beast has devoured him.' We shall see what will become of his dreams!"

But Reuben heard it, and he delivered him out of their hands, and said, "Let us not kill him." And Reuben said to them, "Shed no blood, but cast him into this pit which is in the wilderness, and do not lay a hand on him"—that he might deliver him out of their hands, and bring him back to his father.

So it came to pass, when Joseph had come to his brothers, that they stripped Joseph of his tunic, the tunic of many colors that was on him. Then they took him and cast him into a pit. And the pit was empty; there was no water in it.

It's interesting that this event follows another incident with two of Joseph's brothers. Read Genesis 34. Jacob's sons killed every male in the city of Shechem and plundered it to avenge their sister. No wonder Jacob responded when he heard the report: "You have troubled me by making me obnoxious among the inhabitants of the land ... since I am few in number, they will gather themselves together against me and kill me. I shall be destroyed, my household and I" (v. 30).

Then in chapter 37, Joseph's brothers go to Shechem to tend the flocks. What kind of danger might Joseph have faced in going to Shechem alone considering the massacre his brothers had perpetrated there? What does this say about Joseph's willingness to obey his father when his father sends him out?

_____

_____

_____

_____

Everything had been going so well to this point. But in this moment, it seemed as though Joseph's dreams would never come to pass. Joseph was going through the Pit Test—a test all of us will endure at one time or another.

You know you're experiencing the Pit Test when nothing in your life seems to be going right. Things may have been going smoothly, but then everything goes very wrong all at once. It's easy to get discouraged and depressed because you're in a pit, and it appears there's no way out.

Every one of us will fall into a pit at some point in our lives. The question is, *Are we going to stay in the pit forever, or are we going to pass the Pit Test and move on toward our destiny?*

If you want to know how to get out of the pits of life, it's important to understand how you fall into them.

Reasons You Find Yourself in the Pit

What does John 16:33 tell us about the pits of life?

_____

_____

_____

_____

Pits—the troubles of life—are simply a byproduct of what?

_____

_____

When we find ourselves in a pit, we tend to think we had little to do with how we got there. But if we look inward (in soul searching, not condemnation), we usually find that we have played at least some part in getting ourselves into a pit. What was David's motivation in Psalm 139:23–24?

_____

_____

_____

_____

Define in your own words what a victim mentality is.

_____

_____

_____

_____

Who or what are some things we might blame for any situation or trouble we get into?

_____

_____

_____

_____

In my story about buying the Suburban, I bought it because it was a good deal, despite God telling me not to buy it. Have you ever done something similar? Explain.

_____

_____

_____

_____

How was this resolved, and what is the significance of the timing behind my friend's donation?

_____

_____

_____

_____

Pride and disobedience put me in a pit. Who else could I have blamed?

_____

_____

_____

_____

Describe a time when you found yourself in a pit. Who or what did you blame for the situation? Looking back on that specific situation, what were the real causes?

_____

_____

_____

_____

Do you think Joseph wore his coat with an attitude of pride? Why?

_____

_____

_____

_____

Why do you think Joseph was not out in the fields with his brothers in the first place?

_____

_____

_____

_____

Why do you think Jacob sent Joseph on the journey?

_____

_____

_____

_____

Joseph may have looked like an innocent victim in that pit, but he contributed to the events that put him there.

What's the first thing we need to do when we find ourselves in a pit?

_____

_____

_____

_____

What are some lessons we might learn from Joseph when we are in a pit?

_____

_____

_____

_____

Joseph's father, out of his great love for him, gave him a gift. But here's the problem: Joseph became proud of the gift his father gave him, and he showed it off every chance he got. He started to find his identity in the *gift* that identified him as the favored son, rather than in the *relationship* that made him the favored son. He ended up losing his gift as a result.

What are some examples of finding worth or identity in a gift rather than in the relationship that contributed to receiving the gift?

_____

_____

_____

_____

I mentioned that sometimes Christians boast about having spiritual gifts. How might this type of boasting be received by those *outside* the church?

_____

_____

_____

_____

What happens when we love the gift more than the Giver of the gift?

_____

_____

_____

_____

When God gives us gifts, He doesn't take them back. The Bible tells us the gifts and callings of God are irrevocable; the King James Version says they are "without repentance" (Romans 11:29). This means God does not take back the gifts He has given us, but we can lose them ourselves. We've seen a lot of high-profile pastors and leaders over the years poorly steward their gifts because of pride and a lack of integrity. I wonder how many people have a gift from God but have misappropriated it or aren't able to use it because pride got in the way.

Can you think of a circumstance where a prominent Christian leader lost or squandered their gift because of pride?

_____

_____

_____

_____

How does the end of Joseph's story show how God can restore a gift once lost—both the gift itself and relationships?

_____

_____

_____

_____

Have you ever had a gift (physical or otherwise) restored to you that you thought had been lost forever? Explain. How did that make you feel?

_____

_____

_____

_____

King David went through many periods of failure and extreme distress. Read 1 Samuel 30. What did David have restored in this incident?

_____

_____

_____

_____

When you find yourself in a pit, you may feel that all is lost. But if you cry out to God in humility of heart, He is eager to restore you. The Bible says that if you humble yourself, you will be exalted (see 1 Peter 5:6).

Whatever you have lost, God can restore it if you repent and walk in humility.

Lies of the Pit

We've learned it's dangerous to walk in pride because you can end up in a pit. But we need to understand that the pit itself can also be a dangerous place. That's because of what I call the lies of the pit.

Be assured, any time you fall into a pit you will encounter the lies of the enemy—lies of accusation, lies of hopelessness, and even fabricated evidence. And if you believe his lies, you could stay in the pit indefinitely.

If you want to get out, you will have to learn to discern the enemy's lies and resist them with the truth.

From whom do all lies originate?

_____

_____

_____

_____

The story of the communion server who spilled some juice is an example of a mental pit. Have you ever created a mental pit over some trivial issue or even something that wasn't an issue at all? Explain.

_____

_____

_____

_____

It's important to understand that when you fall into a pit, whether it's one you imagine or one that's real, the devil will immediately accuse you. You'll hear his accusations in your mind. *See, you're no good, or you wouldn't be in this pit. What's more, you'll never be any good! You'll never do anything for God. You'll never get your life straightened out.* Every time you hear condemning thoughts like this, remind yourself of the source, because Satan accuses us, *not* God, and we are commanded to resist him (see James 4:7).

In your own words and experience, how do you resist the devil?

_____

_____

_____

_____

What is the difference between being accused by the enemy and being convicted by the Holy Spirit?

_____

_____

_____

_____

I feel such a burden for you to know God's character, so let me repeat this: God will *never* condemn you.

What accusations and lies might Satan have told Joseph while he was in the pit?

_____

_____

_____

_____

What accusations and lies has the enemy told you?

_____

_____

_____

_____

What does God's truth say about the things the enemy has told you?

_____

_____

_____

_____

Why is it so important to not let our circumstances determine what we believe?

_____

_____

_____

_____

What fabricated evidence was used to get Jacob to believe that Joseph was dead?

_____

_____

_____

_____

Describe your feelings about the actions of Joseph's brothers.

_____

_____

_____

_____

Why is it so easy to fabricate evidence in today's world and so difficult to determine facts from lies?

_____

_____

_____

_____

I share the example of when my son Josh was criticized in a hateful social media post after he preached at Gateway. What happened to the lie when Josh realized the truth?

_____

_____

_____

_____

To overcome the lies of the pit, you must learn to focus on what God says. You must remember that nothing is too hard for God, no matter what evidence the enemy might produce—even when you're in the pit!

Even worse than Satan's false evidence is his biggest lie: "You've messed up too much. It's too late for you. You've messed up so badly you will never fulfill God's destiny for your life."

Have you ever felt like you could not recover after you had messed up? Describe the feeling you had and explain how the situation was resolved. Or, if a situation is not yet resolved, how could it be?

_____

_____

_____

_____

The Bible is a book entirely about restoration. It's filled with stories about people who messed up so badly it seemed even God could do nothing about it—yet He restored every one of them. Nothing is impossible for God! As long as you have breath, it's never too late to call out to God. It doesn't matter what pit you're in. If you call out to God, He can fix it.

The Purpose of the Pit

We can gain important insights from another man in the Bible who messed up and got thrown into a pit.

What was God's assignment to Jonah, and what did Jonah do when God gave him that assignment (see Jonah 1:1–3)?

_____

_____

_____

_____

Tarshish was a city in southern Spain, nearly three thousand miles from the port of Joppa (current-day Jaffa). What does that say about how motivated Jonah was to flee from God?

_____

_____

_____

_____

Jonah 2:1–2 says, "Then Jonah prayed to the LORD his God from the fish's belly. And he said: 'I cried out to the LORD because of my affliction, and He answered me. Out of the belly of Sheol I cried, and You heard my voice.'"

Sheol is an Old Testament word for "the pit," and several translations use the word "pit" here. Jonah had messed up badly and cried out to God from the bottom of his maritime pit. God heard Jonah and delivered him.

That is the real purpose of the pit: to get you to cry out to God so He can deliver you and bring you back into relationship with Him. It's to get you in a place so far down you can't see a way out of it—a place where you can't do it on your own. Because the truth is you actually can't do *anything* on your own. Every breath comes from God! And once you realize this, you will cry out to God, and He will deliver you.

In Jonah 2:1, Jonah refers to the Lord as first "He" (third person) and then "You" (second person). What might this change of words show about what was happening to Jonah's heart and his relationship with God? Explain.

_____

_____

_____

_____

Read Jonah 1:9–17. Look closely at verses 12–14. Why did the crew of the boat throw Jonah into the sea? Who had suggested it? Did Jonah object to this?

_____

_____

_____

_____

_____

Do you think Jonah was suicidal (see also Jonah 4:3) or do you think he expected God to save him through a new appointment—such as when Abraham believed God could bring Isaac back to life (see Hebrews 11:17–19)? Explain.

_____

_____

_____

Jonah 2:5–6 reads:

> The waters surrounded me, even to my soul;
> The deep closed around me;
> Weeds were wrapped around my head.
>
> I went down to the moorings of the mountains;
> The earth with its bars closed behind me forever;
> Yet You have brought up my life from the pit,
> O LORD, my God.

Jonah 1:17 says, "Now the LORD *provided* a huge fish to swallow Jonah" (NIV, emphasis added).

Was the "pit" *only* the inside of the whale, or could it also have been the raging sea into which he had been tossed at the end of chapter 1 or both? Is it fair to say that the huge fish saved Jonah's life? Explain.

_____

_____

_____

_____

Read Acts 27:21–44. Consider the similar maritime experiences of Paul and Jonah. According to verses 24–25, what was the purpose of Paul's pit-like experience? What did that mean for the crew of that ship?

_____

_____

_____

_____

According to verse 43, how did God *provide* for Paul and save his life?

_____

_____

_____

_____

Both Jonah and Joseph had their lives spared when they cried out from the pit. God also spared me from a pit of self-doubt and inadequacy several years ago. No matter what pit you're in—even if you dug it yourself—God is big enough to get you out of it!

Have you ever been in a pit you felt was too big or too deep to escape? What was the result?

_____

_____

_____

_____

Why might our "prayers" sometimes not be adequate to get us out of a pit?

_____

_____

_____

_____

According to the text, how might Joseph's circumstances have begun to change once he repented?

_____

_____

_____

_____

After Joseph's experience in the pit, he was a changed man. He may have failed the Pride Test, but he passed the Pit Test. He then went on to take and pass eight more tests in his life. It's amazing to see how Joseph did the right thing each time he was faced with challenges and temptations.

Read Jonah 4. How did Jonah's attitude about Nineveh change again? What did Jonah want for Nineveh that was not part of God's plan?

_____

_____

_____

_____

How did God chastise and teach Jonah about his prideful attitude? Do you think he passed the Pit Test? Explain.

_____

_____

_____

_____

Redemption from the Pit

God always has a plan. No matter what pit we might be in, God has a plan to get us out of it. And if we dig a little deeper in this story, we can see types and shadows of God's master plan of redemption.

What is God's ultimate plan of redemption?

_____

_____

_____

_____

How is Joseph's brother Reuben a type of Jesus Christ?

_____

_____

_____

_____

How is Joseph a type of Jesus Christ?

_____

_____

_____

_____

What is the important difference between Jesus and Joseph?

_____

_____

_____

_____

Read Matthew 12:39–41. How does Matthew compare Jonah to Jesus?

_____

_____

_____

_____

Jesus Christ died to deliver you from *every* pit, whether you fell into it, were pushed into it, or dug it for yourself. He died so you could have eternal life. He came to deliver you and bring you back into relationship with the Father. Don't let the enemy's lies distract you. Receive what Jesus did for you.

You may have lost the gift God gave you by walking in pride, but God can restore it. Just do what Joseph did. Do what Jonah did. Cry out to God! Say, "God, I'm sorry. I can't get out of this pit on my own. But You can get me out! Show me what You are doing."

When you humble yourself and cry out to God, He will deliver you out of every pit. He will promote you beyond the pit, and He will exalt you so you can walk in the destiny He has planned for you.

For Further Reflection

Job 2:9–10

James 1:2–4

Jonah 2:6 (NIV)

James 1:12

Romans 12:12

Romans 8:18

Key Quotes

Every one of us will fall into a pit at some point in our lives. The question is, Are we going to stay in the pit forever, or are we going to pass the Pit Test and move on toward our destiny?

If we look inward (in soul searching, not condemnation), we usually find that we have played at least some part in getting ourselves into a pit.

When you find yourself in a pit, you may feel that all is lost. But if you cry out to God in humility of heart, He is eager to restore you.

If you want to get out, you will have to learn to discern the enemy's lies and resist them with the truth.

That *is the real purpose of the pit: to get you to cry out to God so He can deliver you and bring you back into relationship with Him.*

CHAPTER THREE

The Palace Test

The Palace Test: Learning Good Stewardship

The Palace Test, also known as the test of stewardship, is the first test Joseph encountered after he was delivered out of the pit.

In Luke 16:10-12, Jesus talked about how someone who is unfaithful in small things cannot be trusted to be faithful in large things. In other words, why should God give you gifts—physical or spiritual—if you cannot be trusted to use them properly?

My story about the incident in the parking garage was an example of a dilemma about doing the right thing in every circumstance, no matter how big or small.

Have you been in a similar situation in the past? How did you respond?

_____

_____

_____

_____

How did the condition of the other car affect my thinking? Describe a situation when a decision you made was influenced by the "relative" damage your action may have caused.

_____

_____

_____

_____

Every one of us would like to move into our glorious destiny, but as we've already seen, every great destiny has great responsibility. God is watching to see whether we can be trusted with little things before He will give us the great things He has in store for us. Until we pass this test, we will never move on into our destiny.

According to Colossians 3:22–25, how should we serve our earthly masters?

_____

_____

_____

_____

Why should we serve that way, and who are we really serving in doing so?

_____

_____

_____

_____

What is a bondservant?

_____

_____

_____

_____

Whatever your job may be, you must understand that you not only work for your employer—you also work for God. And because you work for God, He will reward you. He will promote you and put His blessing on all you do.

This is the reason Joseph was promoted everywhere he went after he was sold into slavery. As Joseph's story progresses, we see that he didn't only work for Potiphar, he didn't only work for the keeper of the prison, and he didn't only work for Pharaoh. Joseph always worked for the Lord (see Colossians 3:23), whatever his circumstances and whoever his boss. And God blessed him.

In what ways are you a bondservant? What relationships do you have or situations are you in that could challenge your stewardship?

_____

_____

_____

_____

Now Joseph had been taken down to Egypt. And Potiphar, an officer of Pharaoh, captain of the guard, an Egyptian, bought him from the Ishmaelites who had taken him down there. The LORD was with Joseph, and he was a successful man; and he was in the house of his master the Egyptian. And his master saw that the LORD was with him and that the LORD made all he did to prosper in his hand. So Joseph found favor in his sight, and served him. Then he made him overseer of his house, and all that he had he put under his authority. So it was, from the time that he had made him overseer of his house and all that he had, that the LORD blessed the Egyptian's house for Joseph's sake; and the blessing of the LORD was on all that he had in the house and in the field. Thus he left all that he had in Joseph's hand, and he did not know what he had except for the bread which he ate. (Genesis 39:1–6)

What rights did Joseph have as a bondservant in Potiphar's house and business?

_____

_____

_____

_____

According to the passage, what was the main reason Joseph was a faithful guardian of Potiphar's business?

_____

_____

_____

_____

Joseph didn't let the injustice of his situation prevent him from serving his master faithfully. Because of this, Potiphar made Joseph the "overseer of his house and all that he had" (v. 4).

What is the origin of this word "overseer"? Describe the significance of that status in Potiphar's household.

_____

_____

_____

_____

If we look ahead, how does Joseph's attitude in this situation compare with his attitude during his time in prison?

_____

_____

_____

_____

"Prosper" Is Not a Bad Word

What are some examples you have seen of people misusing or misunderstanding the word "prosper"?

_____

_____

_____

_____

How many times does the Old Testament use some variation of the word "prospering"? Read some of the passages mentioned in the book.

_____

_____

_____

_____

What does the apostle John mean in 3 John 2 when he says your "soul prospers"?

_____

_____

_____

_____

What do the Hebrew and Greek words for "prospering" mean?

_____

_____

_____

_____

God wants to prosper you in everything you do, just as He prospered Joseph. But it's really up to us whether we will walk in the blessing and favor of God as Joseph did. Four keys caused Joseph to prosper in the palace.

The Key to Prosperity: The Presence of the Lord

As we noted in Genesis 39:1-6, God was with Joseph, and Potiphar noticed God's presence in a tangible way. How do you think Potiphar recognized God's presence?

_____

_____

_____

_____

Find and read other passages in the Bible (Old or New Testament) with the phrase "the Lord was with him." List three of these examples and describe the situation and the result of the Lord's presence.

_____

_____

_____

_____

_____

_____

_____

_____

_____

_____

_____

_____

The Key to the Presence of the Lord: Obedience

How do you feel about the word "obedience"?

_____

_____

_____

_____

Contrast the attitudes and actions of King Saul and David in the stories about their relationship with God as found in 1 Samuel 15 and 1 Samuel 18.

_____

_____

_____

_____

"If you are willing and obedient,
You shall eat the good of the land;
But if you refuse and rebel,
You shall be devoured by the sword";
For the mouth of the LORD has spoken. (Isaiah 1:19–20)

The Lord says in this passage that if you want to "eat the good of the land" (v. 19)—in other words, if you want to prosper—you must be willing and obedient. Then He also says that if you are *not* willing and obedient—but refuse and rebel—you will *not* prosper but will, in fact, be devoured. That seems pretty straightforward: Refuse to obey and expose yourself to the forces of destruction. Or obey and prosper!

God says we must be *willing* and *obedient* to prosper. Our *attitudes* are just as important to God as our *actions*. Have you ever been obedient but not willing? Explain.

_____

_____

_____

_____

According to 2 Chronicles 16:9, what is the real reason God wants us to obey Him willingly?

_____

_____

_____

_____

In Deuteronomy 11:26–28, God sets a choice before His people. How can we describe this simple choice?

_____

_____

_____

_____

God is not talking about our salvation here. Salvation is not by works but by grace that comes through faith in the atoning blood of Jesus Christ. But in these verses in Deuteronomy, God is talking about *being blessed in this life*. He is letting us know that we can choose to be blessed or cursed during our time on this earth. When we choose to obey His commands, we choose blessing. When we disobey, God still loves us, but we don't enjoy the benefits of His presence in the same way.

God is always everywhere. That is His omnipresence. God dwells inside every believer who is born again, through the Holy Spirit. But that's not the presence we're talking about here. These benefits come because of God's *manifest* presence.

What examples have you seen or experienced of God's manifest presence in your life or that of someone else?

_____

_____

_____

_____

How did the presence of the Lord manifest with the Israelites after their exit from Egypt (see Exodus 13:20-22)?

_____

_____

_____

_____

How did God show me what departing from the Lord's presence looks like when I was a young associate pastor? What do you think of this visual?

_____

_____

_____

_____

What did disobedience cost Cain?

_____

_____

_____

How did disobedience cost Adam and Eve? What did they do right after they sinned that shows this effect?

_____

_____

_____

_____

According to Proverbs 28:13, what is required to receive mercy and prosper?

_____

_____

_____

We mentioned King David earlier. He is described as a man after God's own heart, yet he certainly failed to obey at times.

What was the background behind David's fervent prayer in Psalm 51? It may be hard to imagine a circumstance more difficult to redeem than David's transgression with Uriah and Bathsheba. What was restored by David's prayer of repentance and humility?

_____

_____

_____

_____

How does that contrast with what happened to King Saul?

_____

_____

_____

_____

Jonah was obedient when he went to Nineveh and preached redemption to the city, which they gratefully received. Yet, as we mentioned, he still had misgivings, and seemed more interested in justice than redemption. What does this say about willingness and obedience? Have you ever obeyed God but still had misgivings about it? Explain.

_____

_____

_____

_____

The presence of God is what makes you prosper in all you do. And obedience is the key to a life marked by the presence of God. This presents another question.

What is the key to obedience?

The Key to Obedience: Faith

I've actually heard people say, "I know that obedience is important, but I just can't seem to obey God in this certain area. I've tried and tried." You must understand that working out of your own strength—"trying hard"—is not the answer. The key to a life of obedience is simply faith. Because if you truly believe that a life of obedience will produce the blessings of God, you won't *try* to obey Him. You'll *want* to obey Him!

The critical phrase here is "if you believe," because faith is what produces obedience in our lives.

What is the key word in Colossians 3:24 that speaks to this key to obedience?

_____

What are some examples from everyday life where we know—that is, have faith—a result will happen?

_____

_____

_____

_____

Describe in your own words the promises of Isaiah 1:19 and Exodus 19:5. How does that make you feel?

_____

_____

_____

_____

According to Ephesians 6:1–3, what is the promise for children if they obey their parents?

_____

_____

_____

_____

By the way, if things seem as if they have never gone well for you in your life, you may want to ask yourself whether you have failed to honor your parents. The Bible tells us this is "the first commandment with [a] promise" (v. 2). This is a good place to start applying the truths of obedience and blessings. This command does not say to honor your father and mother if they are good people. It does not say to honor your father and mother if they are Christians. It simply says to honor your father and mother so things "may be well with you" (v. 3).

Looking back, have you honored your parents? Why or why not?

_____

_____

_____

_____

Can you identify any areas where honoring (obeying) them has produced fruit in your actions or character?

_____

_____

_____

_____

Can you identify any areas where failing to honor (disobeying) them has produced consequences? Explain.

_____

_____

_____

_____

If you're a parent, what is your attitude toward disciplining your children?

_____

_____

_____

_____

If your children are old enough, can you see some areas where certain discipline was more or less effective? Explain.

_____

_____

_____

_____

As adults, we are not much different from children. We disobey God because we don't really _believe_ we're going to suffer any consequences for our disobedience. And if we really _believed_ God rewards us when we obey Him, we would _want_ to obey. We obey because we believe. We disobey because we don't believe.

What does it mean in Hebrews 3:18–19 that those who do not obey will not "enter His rest"? What was the real, underlying cause of not entering God's rest?

_____

_____

_____

_____

Are there any areas of your spiritual life where lack of belief is holding you back from obeying God's commands? Explain.

_____

_____

_____

_____

God wants every one of us to enter our promised land. Describe in your own words what your promised land is.

_____

_____

_____

_____

The key to God blessing and prospering us is having His presence in our lives. The key to His manifest presence is obedience to His commands, and to walk in obedience to His commands, we must believe. We must have faith.

So what is the key to having faith?

The Key to Faith: Hearing the Word

The key to having faith is in hearing the Word of God. I want to emphasize this: the key to having faith is *not* in *obeying* the Word of God—the key to having faith is in *hearing* the Word of God. Obedience doesn't produce faith. Faith produces obedience. The apostle Paul made it clear in Romans 10:17: "So then faith comes by hearing, and hearing by the word of God." There is something about *hearing* the Word of God that produces faith.

How does hearing the Word of God lead to *doing* God's will (see James 1:22) and living out His Word?

_____

_____

_____

_____

The more of the Word of God you have in you, the more faith you will have. The more faith you have, the more you will obey. The more you obey, the more the presence of God will manifest in your life. And the more you live in the presence of God, the more you will prosper and succeed wherever God has placed you, whether you're a servant in a palace, a manager in an office building, or a stay-at-home parent.

Besides reading the Bible, what are some ways you might hear God's Word?

_____

_____

_____

_____

Jesus tells us more about hearing God's Word in the parable of the soils in Luke 8:12–15, 18:

> The seeds that fell on the footpath represent those who hear the message, only to have the devil come and take it away from their hearts and prevent them from believing and being saved. The seeds on the rocky soil represent those who hear the message and receive it with joy. But since they don't have deep roots, they believe for a while, then they fall away when they face temptation. The seeds that fell among the thorns represent those who hear the message, but all too quickly the message is crowded out by the cares and riches and pleasures of this life. And so they never grow into maturity. And the seeds that fell on the good soil represent honest, good-hearted people who hear God's word, cling to it, and patiently produce a huge harvest.
>
> So pay attention to how you hear. To those who listen to my teaching, more understanding will be given. But for those who are not listening, even what they think they understand will be taken away from them. (NLT)

Jesus describes four results that can happen when we hear the Word. Three of those results are bad—the Word is taken away. They are ones who (1) also listen to the devil, (2) have no roots and cannot withstand testing, or (3) are weak and do not grow and mature. The fourth group consists of those who are willing to keep the Word and *persevere*! (Remember that word *willing*?) That is why Jesus admonishes in verse 18 about "how you hear." The New International Version in verse 18 says to "consider carefully how you listen."

Think of yourself or someone you know who has heard the Word in various ways. Describe which of the four categories of soil in this parable applied to their response and why they might have responded that way.

_____

_____

_____

_____

Simply put, hearing does not mean just being in the room when words are spoken. It does little good to sit in the auditorium wearing noise-canceling headphones. One must actually listen—pay attention to—the words on the page of the Bible, the lyrics of the song being sung, or the message of the preacher or prophet.

Every one of us can prosper, and every one of us can succeed. The way we begin is by hearing the Word of God. So make the Word of God part of your everyday life! Open your mind and heart to *carefully* listen to receive the Word.

In the book, I describe how we bought James an audio copy of the New King James Version of the Bible to replace his old King James Version. The main point is that the time James spent with the Word ultimately led to prosperity. But notice also that the reason we bought James the New King James Version was not so he could have a Bible— he already had all the verses of Scripture in the old version and had listened to them. Rather, I knew the New King James Version would be easier to understand and learn from than the old version. It was just a small example of enabling James to listen *carefully* to receive the Word.

I shared a story about how hearing God's Word in Deuteronomy 11 led to prosperity for Gateway Church. What can you take away from this example?

_____

_____

_____

_____

Why was it important that I persevered, carefully read that chapter again, *and* prayed about it? Has the Lord ever spoken to you multiple times through a well-known Bible verse?

_____

_____

_____

_____

One might also hear the Word through an example of service. Just as the Bible says the existence of God should be evident in creation (see Romans 1:18–21) and that everyone will know we are disciples by our love for one another (see John 13:35), my note to the woman whose car I bumped led to an opportunity to witness to her and her colleagues—to hear the Word through my actions.

Like Joseph, you can live in the favor, blessing, and prosperity of God. God *can* bless you, and He *wants* to bless you.

So be faithful in little things. Be a good employee "as to the Lord" (Colossians 3:23) and a good steward of whatever He has given you. Spend time in God's Word and watch your faith increase. As faith comes, obedience will naturally follow. Hear (carefully), believe (in your heart), and obey (willingly). And when you honor God and walk in obedience to Him—no matter your circumstances or position—He will honor you with His presence. Then His favor and blessings will rest on your life, and like Joseph, you will prosper in all you do.

And then you will know you've passed the Palace Test.

For Further Reflection

1 Peter 4:10

John 14:23

1 Corinthians 4:1

Proverbs 21:20

Psalm 24:1

Key Quotes

God is watching to see whether we can be trusted with little things before He will give us the great things He has in store for us.

God wants to prosper you in everything you do, just as He prospered Joseph.

The presence of God is what makes you prosper in all you do. And obedience is the key to a life marked by the presence of God.

We obey because we believe. We disobey because we don't believe.

The more of the Word of God you have in you, the more faith you will have.

CHAPTER FOUR

The Purity Test

S ome years ago, I preached on the subject of sexual purity at church. I noticed how uncomfortable the topic seemed to make the congregation feel, which was surprising considering how society is saturated with sexual content and seems intent on making us comfortable about sex.

Over the past hundred years, immoral sexual behavior has become so prevalent that even the president of the United States was impeached after lying about his affair with a White House intern in the 1990s. Most people, it seems, couldn't have cared less, implying the president's private behavior had nothing to do with his leadership of our country. Nothing could be further from the truth.

Despite man's opinions, God has spelled out certain truths quite clearly for us in the Bible.

The Purity Test: Sexual Stewardship

Popular culture may declare that sexual morality has nothing to do with character, but God begs to differ. Sexual morality has *everything* to do with character, and character is very important to God. That's why if you want to walk in the destiny God has planned for you, you must understand what He says about sexual purity.

God created us as sexual beings, and He wants each one of us to enjoy a wonderful, fulfilling sex life with our spouse. But as with every other gift God has given us, we have a responsibility to steward this gift in a way that is pleasing to Him. God is watching to see if we will be faithful stewards in this area of our lives. Remember, if we are faithful in little things, God knows He can trust us with much. But if we are unfaithful in little things, God says we will also be unfaithful in much (see Luke 16:10).

What were you taught growing up about sexuality and sex? How did you react to that teaching then, and what do you think of it now?

_____

_____

_____

_____

It's very important to understand this truth because a person who is immoral in this area of his or her life will also be immoral in other areas. A person who cheats on his or her spouse will often also cheat his or her employer (or his or her country). This is not an idea I came up with; it's simply *what God has said in His Word*. Our sexual conduct does matter to God, and that's why it's imperative to be faithful in this area of our lives.

To some degree this is a recent cultural phenomenon in the United States. The 1960s and 1970s were a period associated with the "Sexual Revolution," where free and open sex was promoted. The FDA approval of the first birth control pill in 1960 probably contributed to that, but until 1972, the pill was originally only authorized for married or engaged women.[1] Even then there was an assumption about morality and sex outside marriage. The increase in sexual immorality over the following decades was undoubtedly due to a number of issues.

Character is a foundational issue. Why can we never "only" be sexually immoral?

_____

_____

_____

_____

Why do we lie and act deceptively when we are sexually immoral?

_____

_____

_____

_____

What are some examples you have heard of famous political, corporate, or spiritual leaders being caught up in immorality? What can we learn from their stories?

_____

_____

_____

_____

In God's kingdom, character has everything to do with fitness for leadership. Understand that if we allow any compromise in this area, we are putting our God-given destinies at risk.

Of course, God is a redeemer by nature. If you've fallen in this area and sincerely repent before God, He will forgive you and restore you. But if you *persist* in immorality, you will not step into your destiny. Why? Because God is looking for faithful stewards He can trust wholeheartedly.

This is the Purity Test, and in our hyper-sexualized society, each one of us faces this critical test every day. Thankfully, we can all draw inspiration and insight from the story of Joseph. When faced with great temptation, Joseph passed this test with flying colors! Genesis 39 tells the story.

> Now Joseph was handsome in form and appearance. And it came to pass after these things that his master's wife cast longing eyes on Joseph, and she said, "Lie with me."
>
> But he refused and said to his master's wife, "Look, my master does not know what is with me in the house, and he has committed all that he has to my hand. There is no one greater in this house than I, nor has he kept back anything from me but you, because you are his wife. How then can I do this great wickedness, and sin against God?"
>
> So it was, as she spoke to Joseph day by day, that he did not heed her, to lie with her or to be with her.
>
> But it happened about this time, when Joseph went into the house to do his work, and none of the men of the house was inside, that she caught him by his garment, saying, "Lie with me." But he left his garment in her hand, and fled and ran outside. (Genesis 39:6–12)

While all sin is wrong, the apostle Paul also tells us that sexual sin is different. First Corinthians 6:18–20 says,

Run from sexual sin! No other sin so clearly affects the body as this one does. For sexual immorality is a sin against your own body. Don't you realize that your body is the temple of the Holy Spirit, who lives in you and was given to you by God? You do not belong to yourself, for God bought you with a high price. So you must honor God with your body. (NLT)

In your own words, what does it mean to "sin against your own body"?

_____

_____

_____

_____

How do you "honor God" with your body?

_____

_____

_____

_____

Note what Joseph did to pass this test—*He ran!* Like Paul admonishes the Corinthians to do. Run. That's just what Joseph did, even though he had to leave his garment in Potiphar's wife's hand so he could get away. Joseph knew the wrong done would not only be against Potiphar but against the Lord.

How was this event a test of stewardship in relation to the tenth commandment? What would he avoid coveting, and what did he have to steward?

_____

_____

_____

_____

According to 1 Corinthians 9:27, why is it so important to discipline (control or bring into subjection) our bodies?

_____

_____

_____

_____

Do you struggle with lust? (Be honest. You're not alone. This is a struggle for many people!) How do you think it affects your willingness and desire to obey and follow God?

_____

_____

_____

_____

I struggled with the Purity Test, but God showed me some keys that helped me pass this important test, and I believe they will help you, too. But first, let's talk about why it's imperative to remain pure.

Impurity Will Affect Your Family

If you let impurity become part of your life, it _will_ affect your spouse, your children, and your grandchildren.

The story of David and his family in 2 Samuel 11–13 illustrates this reality. There is adultery, murder, incest, and intrigue. What were the sins David committed in chapter 11? What motivated David to commit those sins?

_____

_____

_____

_____

How do you react to Amnon's treatment of Tamar? What emotion overtook Amnon, and what did he do to Tamar after he took advantage of her?

_____

_____

_____

_____

What are the two reasons for introducing this story? Explain.

_____

_____

_____

_____

Why did David have a blind spot to his kids' impurity?

_____

_____

_____

_____

What does this teach you about the effect of immorality in your own life?

_____

_____

_____

_____

Exodus 34:6-7 talks about the effect of iniquities on generations of family. Lust is an iniquity and dwells in the heart.

What are the differences between sin and iniquity?

_____

_____

_____

_____

Sin is an action. The heart attitude behind the action is iniquity. Adultery is the outward movement, but lust is the inward motivation.

What does this quote mean to you: "What one generation tolerates, the next generation will embrace"?

_____

_____

_____

_____

How might the decades since the sexual revolution show this truth? Give some examples.

_____

_____

_____

_____

_____

_____

_____

Read Isaiah 53:5. How has Jesus set us free from sin *and* iniquity?

_____

_____

_____

_____

Impurity Is Always Lust, Not Love

Impurity is *always* lust, *never* love! If you're in an adulterous relationship, it's not love; it's lust. Potiphar's wife did not love Joseph—she lusted after him. If she loved him, she would not have lied about him and let him sit in prison for ten years.

Most sin is born of selfishness. Why is lust the most selfish sin there is?

_____

_____

_____

_____

Young people are under tremendous pressure from the world to compromise their sexual purity. Our current culture is highly sexualized. But you need to understand the truth. Satan is a liar, and sexual immorality has consequences (and they are different consequences than love produces).

What are some of the potential consequences of sex before marriage?

_____

_____

_____

_____

What is God's motivation behind wanting people to maintain sexual purity?

_____

_____

_____

_____

Who would not want the blessing of God on their sexual relationship with their spouse? When we walk in obedience to God, we have His blessing. But when we walk in disobedience to God, we invite destruction into that area of our lives. The only way to close the door is through repentance.

Some couples who have been married for years also need to understand this because they may have opened the door to destruction before they got married and don't know how to shut it.

Why does premarital sex open the door to dissatisfaction with sex after marriage? Explain.

_____

_____

_____

_____

When I counsel couples who have gone through adultery, I have learned to ask them about this: "I'm not trying to pry, but I need to know so we can shut a door. Did the two of you have premarital sex?" In nearly every case, the answer is "Yes."

What is the sin-induced process that often leads to adultery and divorce? How does it progress?

_____

_____

_____

_____

If you are married, does this apply to you? If so, are you willing to repent and seek forgiveness?

_____

_____

_____

_____

Impurity Will Affect Your Relationship with God

Why and how does immorality negatively affect your relationship with God?

_____

_____

_____

_____

Why is it so difficult—and so destructive—to have to continuously be deceptive and cover up immoral activity?

_____

_____

_____

_____

What do Psalm 66:18 and Proverbs 28:9 tell us about the prayers of someone engaged in deceit?

_____

_____

_____

_____

If you are talking to a spirit with such prayers, what kind of spirit is that likely to be?

_____

_____

_____

_____

When lying and deception become a way of life, what happens to your relationship with the Holy Spirit? Explain.

_____

_____

_____

_____

Read James 1:14–16. What does the apostle James say is the ultimate outcome of deceitful living?

_____

_____

James is pleading with believers not to be deceived, but to let God do a work in this area of their lives. If you're deceived, God is pleading with you to repent, because that's the only way you can have a relationship with Him. You must come to God on His terms, not yours. Repent, renounce your sin, and tell God you want to come back to Him.

Repentance is vital. This is a strong statement, but we all need to hear it: if you let sin thrive in this area of your life, you will *not* fulfill your destiny.

What should you repent of in this area of your life?

_____

_____

_____

_____

Impurity Will Affect Your Future

Satan will try to persuade you that immorality has no real impact on you, your family, or your future. And he can present a convincing case.

Why would Satan's lies look especially convincing to Joseph?

_____

_____

_____

_____

What three things did Joseph stand to lose by yielding to temptation?

_____

_____

_____

_____

What does the metaphor that Solomon uses in Proverbs 7:18-23 say about how serious the impact of adulterous, immoral behavior is?

_____

_____

_____

_____

Speaking of King Solomon, he was certainly a wise man. He was the second son of David and Bathsheba. His wisdom and wealth brough him great riches (see 2 Chronicles 9:1-7). He used that wealth to build the First Temple in Jerusalem. Yet his great wealth also led to some unwise decisions (see 1 Kings 11:1-13).

What was King Solomon's besetting sin in ignoring Deuteronomy 17:17 (see 1 Kings 11:3-8)? What was the result (see vv. 11-13)?

_____

_____

_____

_____

How might the book of Ecclesiastes reflect how Solomon finished his life (see Ecclesiastes 1:2)?

_____

_____

_____

_____

Most of us know the story of Samson, who became a judge of Israel,
known for his great strength. Samson's birth was an answer to prayer
to release Israel from the Philistines (see Judges 13:8, 24). He had been
a judge for twenty years when he also lost sight of his destiny. Read
Judges 13:5 and 16:4–20. What caused Samson's downfall?

_____

_____

_____

_____

Impurity will cost you the presence of God in your life, and it will
cost you your destiny.

So how do we protect ourselves against impurity?

Impurity Begins in the Eye, Not in the Heart

According to Genesis 39:6–7, how did the process of impurity in
Potiphar's wife progress?

_____

_____

_____

_____

What was the fatal first action in King David's sin of adultery (see 2 Samuel 11:2) that was similar to that of Potiphar's wife?

_____

_____

_____

_____

Simply put, what does *looking* inevitably stir up?

_____

The reason Joseph didn't fall when temptation came was because lust was not in his heart, and lust was not in his heart because he had not allowed it into his eyes. *"Don't look"* should become a motto for us all.

List some things we should not allow our eyes to see.

_____

_____

_____

_____

Why is it so much easier now to access immoral content than it was twenty years ago?

_____

_____

_____

_____

What is your reaction to the statistics around the alarming number of people accessing pornography?

_____

_____

_____

_____

How has the nature and stigma of viewing and engaging in pornography changed over the years?

_____

_____

_____

_____

Can you look back and see any effect on your feelings, emotions, or actions related to this issue?

_____

_____

_____

_____

Why is pornography use a problem? Why are these statistics so disturbing? Because people don't want to acknowledge the serious damage pornography does.

According to the studies cited, what are some of the consequences of pornography?

_____

_____

_____

_____

Don't let the enemy fool you! Pornography is an addictive, damaging, and pervasive problem in our society.

What does Psalm 101:3 say about how we should approach looking at things?

_____

_____

_____

_____

What are some practical ways you can prevent temptation to look in the first place?

_____

_____

_____

_____

What is the relationship between looking and the progression of sin as Jesus describes it in Matthew 5:28–29?

_____

_____

_____

Jesus talks in Matthew 6:22–23 about the eye being the source of light. Jesus is saying that what we set before our eyes will eventually end up in our hearts and affect our entire bodies. He says it is our responsibility to let light in.

Go back to chapter 8 in Luke and look at the passage about hearing the Word, which said we should listen carefully. In the middle of that passage, Jesus also spoke about light in verses 16–17:

No one lights a lamp and then covers it with a bowl or hides it under a bed. A lamp is placed on a stand, where its light can be seen by all who enter the house. For all that is secret will eventually be brought into the open, and everything that is concealed will be brought to light and made known to all. (NLT)

Just as we said that hearing involves listening (positive action on the part of the hearer), what does this passage say about our responsibility with the light?

_____

_____

_____

_____

Do you remember the child's song "This Little Light of Mine"? Under what do we *not* hide the light?

_____

_____

_____

_____

How, like Job, can you make a covenant with your eyes?

_____

_____

_____

_____

According to 1 Corinthians 10:13, temptation can *always* be overcome, and God will *always* provide an escape. We just need to remain close to Him every day. We *can* control our looking!

If you are failing in this area, you have not forfeited your destiny, but there are steps you must take to pass this test.

The Importance of Honesty and Accountability

One thing you need to understand is that Satan works in the darkness. So if you have difficulty with sexual purity, you need to expose it and uncover it. Because the more you keep it hidden, the more power you give to Satan.

What is almost always the most important factor that causes suffering in a marriage when there is immorality? Explain.

_____

_____

_____

_____

How can you develop honest accountability with your spouse?

_____

_____

_____

_____

How did Debbie help keep me accountable? Have you ever had to deal with this kind of situation? How did you go about it?

_____

_____

_____

_____

How difficult is it for you to develop accountability with your spouse? With others?

_____

_____

_____

_____

What are the *two key words* to remember when dealing with this issue?

_____

What other avenues of accountability do you have in your life, such as relatives, close friends, or small group at church?

_____

_____

_____

_____

What Is the Answer?

What is the answer to overcoming the temptations that surround us? How can we pass the Purity Test on a continuing basis and be counted faithful to walk in our destiny? We can see the answer by looking once again at the way Joseph passed this test.

Joseph had many opportunities to sin. If lust had been in his heart, eventually he would have fallen. But when the temptation became too great, he ran away. The reason he had the strength to run away is that he had not allowed lust a place in his heart. He had kept lust *out* of his heart by allowing God a place *in* his heart, each and every day. Joseph had learned the secret of walking with God day by day.

Like Joseph, you will encounter temptations daily. And like Joseph, you must deal with those temptations by trusting in God *day by day*. This is the answer to gaining victory in this area.

What are four ways you can rely on God every day?

_____

_____

_____

_____

Why do we know there is hope if we have fallen into sin? What has God done for us, and how should we respond?

_____

_____

_____

_____

Why is it important for us to be careful, even if lust is not an area of temptation for us?

_____

_____

_____

_____

Every one of us must "take heed" to pass the Purity Test. We must cry out to God to help us be a pure people, a holy people. We must lean on Him every day for the grace to walk in purity before Him and run like Joseph did when we're tempted. Because our God has commanded us, "You shall be holy, for I the LORD your God am holy" (Leviticus 19:2).

It's only when we're found faithful in the test of purity that God's presence and blessing can rest upon our lives. It's only then that we can walk in the fullness of the destiny God has planned for each of us.

For Further Reflection

1 Timothy 4:12

Hebrews 13:4

1 Thessalonians 4:3–5

1 Corinthians 6:18

Ephesians 5:5

Key Quotes

Sexual morality has everything to do with character, and character is very important to God.

In God's kingdom, character has everything to do with fitness for leadership.

Sin is an action. The heart attitude behind the action is iniquity. Adultery is the outward movement, but lust is the inward motivation.

When we walk in obedience to God, we have His blessing. But when we walk in disobedience to God, we invite destruction into that area of our lives. The only way to close the door is through repentance.

Impurity will cost you the presence of God in your life, and it will cost you your destiny.

Temptation can always be overcome, and God will always provide an escape.

CHAPTER FIVE

The Prison Test

We must obey God if we want to walk in His blessings, but obedience is no guarantee that bad things will never happen to us. We must do the right thing if we want to have the presence of God in our lives. But sometimes we will do the right thing and still get bad results.

What was the result of Joseph's God-honoring decision as shared in Genesis 39:20?

_____

_____

_____

_____

The Prison Test: Persevering

The Prison Test is about continuing to honor the Lord in your circumstances, even if they're unjust. It could also be called the Perseverance Test because this is the longest of all the tests and can last for years. Every one of us will go through this test at some point in our lives.

What are some examples of when you (or someone you know) have done the right thing and suffered short-term consequences?

_____

_____

_____

_____

What does John 16:33 tell us about life?

_____

_____

_____

_____

What happens to *both* houses in the parable in Matthew 7:24–27?

_____

_____

_____

_____

What is the underlying truth in this parable?

_____

_____

_____

Prison was a horrible place, but the penalty for attempted rape in Egypt was death, so it was actually by the grace of God that Joseph ended up in prison rather than an early grave. I personally believe that Potiphar suspected his wife was lying. He was probably well aware of her true character, and he also knew the character of Joseph. He wanted to spare Joseph's life, but he had to save face, so he had Joseph thrown into prison.

According to Genesis 39:22–23, how did Joseph grow while in prison? What status did he achieve?

_____

_____

_____

_____

Romans 5 says much about tribulation and is the basis for much of this lesson:

> And not only that, but we also *glory in tribulations*, knowing that tribulation produces perseverance; and perseverance, character; and character, hope. Now hope does not disappoint, because the love of God has been poured out in our hearts by the Holy Spirit who was given to us. (vv. 3–5, emphasis added)

What does the Greek word typically used for "glory" (*doxa*) mean?

_____

_____

_____

_____

What is a good translation for the Greek word used for "glory" in this verse (*kauchaomai*)?

_____

_____

_____

_____

What does the Greek root word of *kauchaomai* mean?

_____

_____

_____

_____

Would you say you can rejoice in tribulation? Why or why not? Explain.

_____

_____

_____

_____

How do we reach the point where we actually *wish* for tribulation and rejoice in it when it comes? The answer can be found in understanding what God says about the way tribulation works in our lives.

Tribulation Produces Perseverance

Romans 5:3 tells us, "Tribulation produces perseverance." According to the Bible, there is no other way to get it. So why not allow tribulation to produce perseverance, as God says it will? Why not allow tribulation to do a valuable work of God in our lives?

In John 15, Jesus talks about two vines. Explain the difference between the two types of cutting, based upon whether or not we produce fruit.

_____

_____

_____

_____

What was God's plan for pruning Joseph?

_____

_____

_____

According to James 1:2–5, how do we get patience?

_____

_____

_____

_____

Why can we "count it all joy" when we go through a trial?

_____

_____

_____

_____

What happens when we let "perseverance finish its work" (v. 4 NIV)?

_____

_____

_____

_____

What is the key feature of waiting that shows patience?

_____

_____

_____

_____

I hate the spinning wheel that pops up when you're waiting for a computer program to open—I call it the "spiral of death." This small thing has a unique way of exasperating me to no end. I'm still working on developing patience for it.

What things in everyday life test your patience? Explain.

_____

_____

_____

_____

How are patience and perseverance alike?

_____

_____

_____

_____

How are they different?

_____

_____

_____

_____

When a trial goes on for a long time—when months turn into years and still you must stand in faith while the enemy attacks you with thoughts of doubt and hopelessness—it takes more than patience to endure. It takes perseverance.

How long did Joseph go through tribulation?

_____

What other Bible characters had to persevere for as long as or longer than Joseph? How long did their tribulations last and what was at the end of each?

_____

_____

_____

_____

_____

_____

Perseverance Produces Character

According to the formula in Romans 5:3-4, tribulation produces perseverance, and perseverance produces character.

How do we define character? Expand on the definition of character with some of your own thoughts.

_____

_____

_____

_____

What do you think about the idea that your character can be developed only through perseverance?

_____

_____

_____

_____

Why will God not let you step into your destiny before a certain level of character is developed?

_____

_____

_____

_____

What factors should you consider when deciding whether to intervene to help someone in a difficult situation? Who should be your guide? Explain.

_____

_____

_____

_____

Why did Jesus need to learn obedience and through what did He learn it (see Hebrews 2:18; 5:8)?

_____

_____

_____

_____

What is the relationship or progression between enduring trials and character?

_____

_____

_____

_____

How have you seen this play out in your life or the life of someone you know?

_____

_____

_____

_____

One way challenging seasons work in our lives is by causing deep character flaws to emerge. We can see this happening in Joseph's situation. He had God's favor on his life along with tremendous, God-given leadership ability, but God still wanted to work through part of Joseph's character.

When Jacob gave Joseph the special gift of the coat, Jacob grew attached to it and relied upon it. What happened when Joseph used God's gift to interpret dreams for the butler and baker who were in prison with him? What favor did Joseph ask of the butler (see Genesis 40:12–15)?

_____

_____

_____

_____

How long did it take before Joseph was let out of prison? What did Joseph hope would occur from his interpretation?

_____

_____

_____

_____

Do you think the *baker* was as pleased as the butler was with Joseph's interpretation of *his* dream?

_____

_____

_____

_____

Have you ever asked for favor from someone in exchange for your blessing or assistance? (Or has that happened to you?) When do you feel that might be appropriate or not? Explain.

_____

_____

_____

_____

What was the character flaw God wanted Joseph to see from this lesson?

_____

_____

_____

_____

Joseph learned that his own abilities were not enough. It's the same lesson many of us have to learn. God is the *only* one who can promote us and deliver us. We must stop trying to manipulate situations and instead let God work through our surrender, obedience, and reliance on Him. It's only during trials and tribulation we start to see things from God's perspective.

Perseverance is difficult, even for a "friend" of God. Moses waited forty years in Midian before returning to Egypt to lead the Israelites to freedom. Then after they left their enslavement, their constant grumbling during the wilderness journey finally got to Moses at a place called Meribah (which means "quarreling"). The people were lacking water. Read Numbers 20:7–12.

What did the Lord command Moses to do to produce water at Meribah? What did he do instead?

_____

_____

_____

_____

How did God punish Moses and Aaron? Do you think the punishment was excessive?

_____

_____

_____

_____

What practices, tools, and resources do we have for learning how to see things from God's perspective so we can handle troubles when they come?

_____

_____

_____

_____

When we respond the right way to trials, character is being developed in our lives. *And character is simply doing the right thing, no matter your circumstances.*

As character is developed, something wonderful happens: we begin to have hope.

Character Produces Hope

Describe how character works to produce hope.

_____

_____

_____

_____

What are the three tactics Satan used multiple times to attack Joseph?

_____

_____

_____

_____

_____

_____

_____

_____

_____

_____

_____

_____

Despite Satan's tricks, Joseph continued wearing coats (I think!). He continued doing a good job and stewarding what was in front of him. And he continued interpreting dreams, which opened the door for him to step into his destiny.

Put yourself in Joseph's shoes during those thirteen years of waiting. How would you have felt and reacted?

_____

_____

_____

_____

Hope is not that God will deliver you *from* your circumstances. Hope is the knowledge that God will walk with you *through* your circumstances. How can you apply this truth to a situation in your life right now?

_____

_____

_____

_____

"Hope deferred makes the heart sick" (Proverbs 13:12). What would be a better interpretation of this verse?

_____

_____

_____

_____

Deferred hope is misplaced hope. And when you're going through a long and difficult trial, it can easily turn into disappointment. You must not allow that to happen. You must keep trusting God and hoping in Him. For those of us who have walked through long tribulations, this is sometimes easier said than done. But you must persevere and let Him show you His perspective.

In what circumstance or area of your life right now should you lean on hope in God and not on a change of circumstances? Explain.

_____

_____

_____

_____

Why can you have hope *right now* about those circumstances?

_____

_____

_____

_____

What are the four things hope helps us believe?

_____

_____

_____

_____

Hope Produces Appointments

Romans 5:5 tells us what hope does *not* do: *"Hope does not disappoint"* (emphasis added).

"Disappoint" is the opposite of "appoint." So the word "disappoint-ment" means that an appointment has been missed. If you say, "I was disappointed," it means you missed an appointment with something you were hoping for. Conversely, hope "appoints."

What types of appointments does hope produce?

_____   _____

What are divine appointments?

_____

_____

_____

_____

What were some of Joseph's divine appointments?

_____

_____

_____

_____

Can you think of some divine appointments of other Bible figures?

_____

_____

_____

_____

There are people all around you who need God, and God wants you to minister to those people. But if your focus is on your own problems and trials, you'll walk right past opportunities to minister to the needs of others.

Look at some of your past circumstances and relationships. Did you experience any divine appointments? If so, what did you learn? And what might have happened had you missed them?

_____

_____

_____

_____

_____

_____

_____

_____

Look at your current circumstances and relationships. Can you see any potential divine appointments? If so, what are they and how will you respond to them?

_____

_____

_____

_____

_____

_____

_____

_____

Joseph didn't let his brothers, Potiphar's wife, or the butler mess up his destiny. What choice did he make to make sure that was the case?

_____

Who is the only one who can thwart, hinder, or delay your destiny?

_____

What are the four ways that Joseph is a type of Christ? Explain.

_____

_____

_____

_____

_____

_____

_____

_____

_____

_____

_____

_____

_____

_____

_____

Here's my word for you: even if other people don't keep their word, even if other people forget you, God never will. God will always keep His Word, and He will always remember you.

God worked through a divine appointment in the parking lot to open up opportunities for me to preach and minister alongside James Robison. What was the result? What is often the result of a divine appointment?

_____

_____

_____

_____

The Prison Test is about doing the right thing even when you're falsely accused, even when you're thrown in prison, even when you're waiting a long time for your circumstances to change.

It may seem like an eternity, and you may even start to wonder, "Is God really faithful?" Just know that God *is* faithful. And He will use the Prison Test to develop perseverance and His character in your life. And the reward will be beyond what you can ever imagine.

> Blessed is the one who *perseveres* under trial because, having stood the test, that person will receive the crown of life that the Lord has promised to those who love him. (James 1:12 NIV, emphasis added)

For Further Reflection

Revelation 2:10

Jeremiah 17:7–8

Philippians 3:13–14

Hebrews 10:36

Romans 15:13

Key Quotes

So why not allow tribulation to produce perseverance, as God says it will? Why not allow tribulation to do a valuable work of God in our lives?

God is the only one who can promote us and deliver us.... It's only during trials and tribulation that we start to see things from God's perspective.

Hope is not that God will deliver you from your circumstances. Hope is the knowledge that God will walk with you through your circumstances.

There are people all around you who need God, and God wants you to minister to those people.

It may seem like an eternity, and you may even start to wonder, "Is God really faithful?" Just know that God is faithful.

CHAPTER SIX

The Prophetic Test

The Bible tells us plainly that when God wants to create something, He *speaks*.

What are some things God spoke into existence in Genesis 1?

_____

_____

_____

_____

What happens when God speaks something forth?

_____

_____

_____

_____

What did God tell Moses to do to the rock in Numbers 20:8?

_____

_____

_____

_____

God has a plan for every one of us, just as He did for Joseph. And as we have just seen, when God has a plan for something, He *speaks*. That means God has *already spoken* His plan over each one of us. He has *already spoken* a specific word over your life, and He has *already spoken* a specific word over mine. And when He spoke, the power was released to carry us toward the destiny He has planned for us.

How does it make you feel that God has already spoken over your destiny and released the power to carry you toward that destiny?

_____

_____

_____

_____

The Prophetic Test: Finding God's Word for Your Life

How long was it from the time God gave me my ministry vision until we planted Gateway Church? What does that tell you? What immediately confirmed my vision?

_____

_____

_____

_____

What events reconfirmed my vision when we planted Gateway?

_____

_____

_____

_____

Has God ever confirmed a word or vision for you? Explain.

_____

_____

_____

_____

God has called each one of us for a specific purpose. There is no one else who can do what God has called you to do; there is no one else who can do what God has called me to do. But it's up to us to discover the specific words God has spoken over our lives. And it's up to us to believe the prophetic words God has spoken and then obey Him.

That's what the Prophetic Test—the test of God's Word—is all about: will we believe God's words and stand on them, come what may?

What does "prophesy" mean?

_____

_____

_____

_____

God spoke to me in certain ways. What are some other ways God can speak to us?

_____

_____

_____

_____

What are some ways God has spoken to you or to someone you know well?

_____

_____

_____

_____

Have you been able to see some results of those prophecies yet? Explain.

_____

_____

_____

_____

Explain the difference between the two Greek words translated "word" in Psalm 105:19—*dabar* and *imrah.*

_____

_____

_____

_____

Prophetic words tend to test our *faith*, but the literal Word of God, the Bible, tests our *character*. What does that mean in your own words?

_____

_____

_____

_____

Answer these questions in your own words: Do you test the Bible, or does the Bible test you? Do you judge the Bible, or does the Bible judge you?

_____

_____

_____

_____

Right now, whether you know it or not, you are being tested by the Word of God. It is testing your character. Whether you reach your destiny or fail to reach your destiny is directly related to how well you know God's Word.

What is an area of your life where God's Word might be testing you right now? Explain.

_____

_____

_____

_____

What are some examples of things people might need to change before they achieve their destiny because those actions don't line up with the Word of God? Note the related Bible verses.

_____

_____

_____

_____

Know What the Bible Says

The only way to know what the Bible says—what God says—is to read and study it. So read it, listen to it, meditate on it, memorize it, and obey it. As a friend of mine says, "If you're a Christian, you might as well face it: sooner or later, you're going to have to read the Bible!"

If you read ten chapters a day in the Bible, how long would it take to read it through?

_____

_____

_____

_____

Are you or have you in the past engaged in a plan to read through the Bible in a certain period of time? How does that work for you?

_____

_____

_____

_____

Do you struggle to read the Bible regularly? What things can you do to help you read or listen to the Bible?

_____

_____

_____

_____

Are there some parts of the Bible that are more difficult to read through than others? Why do you think that is?

_____

_____

_____

_____

I encourage you to ask the Holy Spirit to renew in you a passion for His Word. As you read or listen to the Bible, ask God questions about things you don't understand or ask Him to give you His perspective on a Scripture. He is faithful to answer!

What do the following verses say about the Bible?

Proverbs 4:20–22 (NIV)

_____

_____

Hebrews 4:12

_____

_____

2 Timothy 3:16–17

_____

_____

In what ways can you make the Bible fun?

_____

_____

_____

_____

Read Genesis 22:20–24. Who were Uz and Buz?

_____

_____

_____

_____

There are commentaries that can help expound on biblical text, but there are also other useful resources to help you study God's Word. There are parallel Bible versions that let you compare different translations side by side. Or if you're interested in words in the original language, there are interlinear versions. The Greek-English New Testament Interlinear Bible is available in several translations. There are also online resources that have both Greek and Hebrew interlinear text.[1] Study Bibles, available in several translations, contain intertextual references and notes to help guide you to various passages and topics. The *Fresh Start Bible* includes a variety of explanatory and supplementary materials to enhance your study.[2]

Which of these additional resources do you have access to or have you used? Which do you find most useful?

_____

_____

_____

_____

Joseph didn't have the written word of God. He lived several hundred years before Moses, who was born in the late fourteenth century BC. Moses, of course, is considered the "writer" of the initial Old Testament Scriptures (the first five books, known as the Torah or Pentateuch), which, along with the rest of the Hebrew Scriptures, were written on scrolls and compiled over the next thousand or so years. These written versions were kept in the Temple in Jerusalem.

The first known written words of Scripture, of course, were the tablets of stone containing the Ten Commandments, given by God to Moses on Mt. Sinai.

Read Exodus 31:18. How was the first set of tablets written?

_____

_____

_____

_____

Read Exodus 32:19. What happened to that first set of tablets and why?

_____

_____

_____

_____

Read Exodus 34:1–4. How were the tablets replaced?

_____

_____

_____

_____

Speaking of Moses, according to Numbers 12:6–8 and Exodus 33:11, how was Moses more than just a prophet? How does that speak to you?

_____

_____

_____

_____

While the primary recording and transmission of God's Word during that period was the passing down of oral tradition and stories, we see at least one example in the Old Testament where the written Word of God came into play in a powerful way. Read 2 Kings 22.

According to this account, what happened when Hilkiah, the High Priest under King Josiah, discovered the written word (the Book of the Law) "in the house of the LORD" (v. 8)? (Read through the end of chapter 22.)

_____

_____

_____

_____

What does this passage say about the character and heart of King Josiah?

_____

_____

_____

_____

What does this passage say about the power of the written Word of God?

_____

_____

_____

_____

Read Matthew 4:4, 7, 10. How did Jesus respond to Satan's temptations? What does this say about how we should respond to temptation?

_____

_____

_____

_____

The Bible is God's Word. And until your dream comes to pass, God's Word is testing you. It's testing your character. Remember, testing means "to refine, prove, or purify." God is not testing you so you'll fail. He's testing you to help you become stronger in your conviction and in your character. Are you a man or woman of God? Can you be trusted with the destiny He has planned for you? God's Word will build your faith and bring you to your destiny.

God Still Speaks Today

We are very blessed to have the Bible. Joseph didn't have the written Word of God. All he had was the word God put in his heart—the prophetic word of God. And since that was all he had, I believe he held on to it tightly. But we are doubly blessed today. We are blessed to have God's written Word in the Bible, which is our standard, and we must hold on to it. We are also blessed to have God's prophetic word, and we must hold on to that as well.

Consider the story about Pastor Olen Griffing at Shady Grove Church. Why do you think some Christians have a problem with the idea that God might speak through someone who prophesies?

_____

_____

_____

_____

What does 1 Thessalonians 5:19–21 teach us about the truth of God speaking today?

_____

_____

_____

_____

Prophetic Words Are Only Part of the Puzzle

What does 1 Corinthians 13:9 tell us about our knowledge of prophecy?

_____

_____

_____

_____

Why can't we prophesy perfectly?

_____

_____

_____

_____

What does 1 Corinthians 14:32 tell us about prophecy?

_____

_____

_____

_____

How did the story about my end-of-the-year dream illustrate this principle?

_____

_____

_____

When we're listening to various pastors and speakers on television or YouTube, for example, we shouldn't tune in to watch only those who strike the "right chord" for us at that moment. What question should you ask God about the messages you watch or hear?

_____

_____

_____

_____

How did Joseph's original dream only portray part of his destiny?

_____

_____

_____

_____

Prophetic Words Are to Be Judged

One time, someone shared with me a word he felt was from God. The only problem was I had about ten Scriptures that proved it couldn't be a word from God.

He said, "But Pastor, I have a word!"

So I picked up my Bible and said, "I have one, too. And if your word doesn't line up with this Word, it can't be from God."

Against what should we judge all prophetic words?

_____

_____

_____

_____

How does 1 Corinthians 14:29 apply?

_____

_____

_____

_____

Why are we to judge, or test, them?

_____

_____

_____

_____

What did the pastor at whose church I spoke mean by saying I prophesied "with a clean screen"?

_____

_____

_____

_____

How We Judge Prophecy

We Judge Prophecy by the Word of God

So how do we judge prophecy? The first way is by testing, or comparing, it against the Word of God. The written Word of God is always our authority, and God's true prophetic words are always confirmed by God's written Word. You can't test a prophecy against itself—you have to prove it with the Word of God. (Remember, the word for "test" can also mean "prove.")

God makes this plain in Deuteronomy 13. He warns us that there will be prophecies that contradict His Word and that these false prophecies will sometimes even be accompanied by signs and miracles.

> If there arises among you a prophet or a dreamer of dreams, and he gives you a sign or a wonder, and the sign or the wonder comes to pass, of which he spoke to you, saying, "Let us go after other gods"—which you have not known—"and let us serve them," you shall not listen to the words of that prophet or that dreamer of dreams, for the LORD your God is testing you to know whether you love the LORD your God with all your heart and with all your soul. (vv. 1-3)

What are the obvious signs that the prophecy in this passage is not from God?

_____

_____

_____

_____

What does God say He is doing to us in these situations?

_____

_____

_____

_____

What will it look like when we pass that test?

_____

_____

_____

_____

Have you ever received a word that didn't line up with God's Word? How did you know?

_____

_____

_____

_____

There's a reason I positioned this chapter in the middle of the book. It's because the Prophetic Test is often in the middle of the journey toward your destiny.

As you go through trials to reach your destiny, will you hold fast to God's Word? No matter what you hear, see, or experience, will you be faithful to the word God has spoken? Will you hold fast to God's Word, no matter what your circumstances might be saying?

We Judge Prophecy by our Inward Witness

The second way we judge prophecy is by our inward witness—by holding it up to what God is saying to us in our own hearts. After all, the Bible says, "The Spirit Himself bears witness with our spirit" (Romans 8:16).

What do you think this verse means?

_____

_____

_____

_____

What do you do when you hear a prophetic word that does not contradict God's Word, but doesn't seem to agree with what the Holy Spirit has been saying to you personally?

_____

_____

_____

_____

What does it mean to judge prophecy by the faith of God?

_____

_____

_____

_____

How and why might this be more difficult than judging prophecy by the Word of God?

_____

_____

_____

_____

Describe how Jeremiah's prophecy to the Rechabites in Jeremiah 35 was a test. What prophecies did they consider, and which did they obey?

_____

_____

_____

_____

Were they wrong to "disobey" the prophet Jeremiah? Explain.

_____

_____

_____

_____

Every Word from God Is Submitted to the God of the Word

What did Jonah say to the people of Nineveh in Jonah 3:4?

_____

_____

_____

_____

What happened when the forty days passed?

_____

_____

_____

_____

What happened when the people of Nineveh repented? What does verse 10 say that God did?

_____

_____

_____

_____

Why was Jonah not happy with this result? What principle does this demonstrate?

_____

_____

_____

_____

What caused the change in the result of Isaiah's prophecy to Hezekiah in Isaiah 38:1–5?

_____

_____

_____

_____

What is the difference between a conditional prophecy and an unconditional prophecy? What does a conditional prophecy test?

_____

_____

_____

Whether or not you end up at your destination depends on how well you go through these tests. What happens if we fail one? What is God's heart for us as we go through these tests?

_____

_____

_____

_____

Hold On to Prophetic Words

Throughout our lives, we will encounter circumstances that seem to contradict the words God has spoken over us. One of the most important things we can do if we want to pass the Prophetic Test is simply to hold on—hold on to the words God has spoken to us! Because there will be many opportunities to let go of those words or stop believing that what God said will come to pass.

In 2020, God once again confirmed the prophecy I had heard years earlier regarding the number of people Gateway Church would reach. But I had to hold on to that prophecy. What should you declare in times of doubt about a prophecy for your life that may be long in coming?

_____

_____

_____

_____

What did the apostle Paul tell the church in Thessalonica about prophecies (see 1 Thessalonians 5:20–21)?

_____

_____

_____

_____

In Philippians 3:12, what does Paul say is required to lay hold of our destiny?

_____

_____

_____

_____

Describe in detail what Paul means when he says to "press on."

_____

_____

_____

_____

How might that be like what James said in James 1:3-4, 12?

_____

_____

_____

_____

According to Paul's charge to Timothy in 1 Timothy 1:18-20, how important is it to take hold of those prophecies and what do we do with them?

_____

_____

_____

_____

What does Paul's story about Hymenaeus and Alexander show about what happens when people reject the prophetic words of God? Explain.

_____

_____

_____

_____

What does the story of my daughter, Elaine, show about holding on to prophecies?

_____

_____

_____

_____

God has a destiny for your life. He has someone He wants you to engage. He has someone He wants you to reach. He has a ministry for you, even if it is not a vocational ministry. So press on to that destiny God has promised. Hold on to the prophetic word of God, no matter what happens. When you do that, you will pass the Prophetic Test. And one day you will step into your destiny. One day you will see every word God has spoken over your life come to pass.

What is a ministry or goal about which God may be speaking to you prophetically?

_____

_____

_____

_____

For Further Reflection

2 Peter 1:21

1 Corinthians 14:1–3

2 Peter 2:1–3

Acts 13:27

Revelation 1:3

Key Quotes

God has a plan for every one of us, just as He did for Joseph. And as we have just seen, when God has a plan for something, He speaks.

It's up to us to discover the specific words God has spoken over our lives. And it's up to us to believe the prophetic words God has spoken and then obey Him.

God's Word is testing your character. Remember, testing means "to refine, prove, or purify." God is not testing you so you'll fail. He's testing you to help you become stronger in your conviction and in your character.

We are blessed to have God's written Word in the Bible, which is our standard, and we must hold on to it. We are also blessed to have God's prophetic word, and we must hold on to that as well.

The written Word of God is always our authority, and God's true prophetic words are always confirmed by God's written Word.

Hold on to the prophetic word of God, no matter what happens.

CHAPTER SEVEN

The Power Test

When our daughter, Elaine, was a little girl, it was not uncommon for me to walk into a room and find all her dolls neatly lined up, while she dictated orders to them. She would say, "Now you go over there, and you go here; you do this, and you do that." What struck me the most about this scene was how even a small child could express the inward desire to rule over the world around her—even if her authority extended only to her dolls!

Have you ever noticed children exercising power or authority over their siblings or inanimate objects? What did you think of that at the time?

_____

_____

_____

_____

Describe in your own words how Matthew 20:26 and 1 Timothy 3:1 show how God wants us to think about power.

_____

_____

_____

_____

Read Genesis 1:27–28. In what ways are humans to exercise power over their environment? For what purposes?

_____

_____

_____

_____

The Power Test: Learning to Steward Your God-Given Authority

God created us to have power, and He wants to give His power to us, but He is looking for those who can be trusted with it. What will we do with the power He gives us? Will we use it wisely as His stewards on this earth?

This is the Power Test. How is this test different from the first six tests?

_____

_____

_____

_____

Why can responding to success and God's blessing be as much of a test as tribulation can? Explain.

_____

_____

_____

_____

What specific blessings or perks of power can be difficult to navigate? In what specific areas is the Power Test different?

_____

_____

_____

_____

_____

_____

_____

It's what you do with the power and blessings of God that is the true test of your character. This is the essence of the Power Test.

What will happen if believers don't have the character necessary to handle blessings or authority?

_____

_____

_____

_____

Have you ever thought you had few or no areas of your life in which you have power or authority? What areas of your life can you identify where you can exercise power or authority?

_____

_____

_____

_____

What event prompted Joseph's release from prison after more than a decade?

_____

_____

_____

_____

What part did the butler play? What did the butler mean when he said, "I remember my faults this day"?

_____

_____

_____

_____

Other than the fact that Joseph was preparing for a meeting, what might be the significance of Scripture recording that "he shaved, changed his clothing, and came to Pharaoh" (Genesis 41:14)?

_____

_____

_____

_____

Read Genesis 41:37–44 again. What were the specific trappings of power that Pharaoh bestowed upon Joseph? What did each of them represent?

_____

_____

_____

_____

_____

_____

_____

_____

_____

_____

_____

The Power Test Comes Suddenly

The Power Test often comes suddenly. Have you ever been in a situation where your circumstances improved significantly and quickly? If so, how did that make you feel (especially the immediate response), and how did you respond?

_____

_____

_____

_____

_____

_____

_____

Power Comes from God

Psalm 62:11 tells us power comes from God: "God has spoken once, twice I have heard this: That power belongs to God." This verse is saying that if we have power, it came from God. He is the only One who can give us power.

Describe the extraordinary irony of Pilate's response to Jesus in John 19:10–11.

_____

_____

_____

_____

Did Pilate in fact have power over Jesus' humanity—in the sense of the legal authority Pilate held as the representative of Caesar? Explain.

_____

_____

_____

_____

How might what Jesus said in Mark 12:17 apply to this circumstance: "Render to Caesar the things that are Caesar's, and to God the things that are God's"?

_____

_____

_____

_____

Like so many of the other tests, this test is also about stewardship. God is looking for people He can trust to steward His power. Power isn't ours to own, and it can be taken away just as quickly as it is given. God wants us to recognize that all power comes from Him, and He wants us to walk in humility.

How Do We Receive Power?

Read Mark 9:35, Matthew 16:25, and Luke 6:38. What spiritual principle do these verses illustrate and how do you apply that principle to power?

_____

_____

_____

_____

How do James 4:10 and 1 Peter 5:5–6 make this principle clear?

_____

_____

_____

_____

What does it mean that God will "exalt [us] in due time" (v. 6)?

_____

_____

_____

_____

How does the football metaphor show the "position" and attitude God wants us to take?

_____

_____

_____

_____

How did the example of my friend with a prophetic gift show the need for humility? Why could he prophesy so easily the first night and not the second?

_____

_____

_____

_____

What factors or characteristics made Joseph a prime candidate for pride?

_____

_____

_____

_____

How does Genesis 41:15–16 show Joseph's humility? To whom did Joseph give credit up front?

_____

_____

_____

_____

Why do people tend to be drawn to leaders or successful people who are humble and avoid those who are arrogant, conceited, and prideful? How do you feel about such people? Explain.

_____

_____

_____

_____

I'm sure you've heard someone say the phrase, "It's all God!" This expression has made its way through Christian circles for a long time, and although I appreciate the heart behind wanting to give the Lord credit, I think it sometimes swings the pendulum too far into false humility.

What should our response to praise be?

_____

_____

_____

_____

Have you ever heard the winner of a sports contest give all praise to God for enabling their victory? What do you think when a player says that? Did God help the other team lose?

_____

_____

_____

_____

What Is the Purpose of Power?

The Bible tells us God gave power to Jesus when Jesus walked this earth. Acts 10:38 says, "God anointed Jesus of Nazareth with the Holy Spirit and with power, who went about doing good and healing all who were oppressed by the devil, for God was with Him."

What was the purpose of Jesus having power? What did He do with that power?

_____

_____

_____

_____

For what good purpose specifically did God give Joseph power at this point in his life?

_____

_____

_____

_____

God's heart is always for people, so God's power is *always* given to help people. That's what power is for, and God wants us to remember that.

According to Deuteronomy 8:17–18, what was the specific and profound eternal purpose for which God gave Israel the power to get their great wealth?

_____

_____

_____

_____

According to the book, what is the purpose of God's covenant?

_____

_____

_____

_____

You see, God owns all the resources in the world—actually, the *universe*. He even owns Mars! One day when Elon Musk gets there, it will say "Property of God." In one hand, God has all the resources. And in the other, He has all the hurting people—all the hungry, broken people who need the Good News, food, money, medicine, and hope. And what's in the middle? *We are.*

How might we describe this principle in simple business terms?

_____

_____

_____

_____

How are we like the distributors in the middle of this imagery, supporting God's supply chain?

_____

_____

_____

_____

Expand upon your answer in the context of Christian stewardship.

_____

_____

_____

_____

What or whom does God have in mind every time He promotes us or gives us a position of influence?

_____

_____

_____

_____

Why did God bless Gateway Church with land, facilities, and resources? Why do you think has God blessed you in certain areas?

_____

_____

_____

_____

Read 2 Corinthians 12:7–10. What does this passage say about power and its relationship to "weakness"? Explain.

_____

_____

_____

_____

Daniel, another well-known Bible character, is an example of how power comes to those who obey God. Consider what the prophet Daniel achieved during the period Israel was in Babylonian captivity and how he achieved it. His story and the fulfillment of his destiny takes place over about seventy years.

What do Daniel 1:19–20 and 5:11 say about Daniel?

_____

_____

_____

_____

What does Daniel 1:17 tell us about Daniel that is similar to the gift Joseph is known for?

_____

_____

_____

_____

What does Daniel 4:8–9 say is the source of Daniel's power to interpret dreams?

_____

_____

_____

_____

What did Daniel do in Daniel 2:24–49 in addition to interpreting Nebuchadnezzar's dream (see v. 26)?

_____

_____

_____

What did Nebuchadnezzar give Daniel in v. 48?

_____

_____

_____

What did Belshazzar give Daniel in Daniel 5:29 for interpreting the "writing on the wall"? How is this similar to Joseph's story?

_____

_____

_____

Daniel 6 is the story of Daniel in the lion's den. It was King Darius' appointment of Daniel in verse 1 as one of the administrators of the satraps (rulers of the kingdom) that caused those leaders to scheme and have Darius decree that no one could pray to anyone other than Darius—a law that Daniel did not obey. After being released from the lion's den, verse 28 says, "Daniel prospered in the reign of Darius [the Mede] and in the reign of Cyrus the Persian."

Daniel was a youth, probably in his early teens, when chosen by Nebuchadnezzar. How old would he have been during the reign of King Darius near the end of Babylonian captivity seventy years later?

_____

Under how many kings did Daniel have great power and prosper?

_____

_____

_____

_____

Read Matthew 11:29 and 5:5. How can meekness and power be related?

_____

_____

_____

Power is not a bad thing. It's a good thing, and it comes from God. Power is given for the purpose of helping others. You may not be second in command of all of Egypt like Joseph, have high leadership positions under several kings like Daniel, or even know how much influence you have, but you do have influence. The Power Test is all about recognizing that any power, influence, or success we experience is not for our own purposes. We may work hard and respond well to God's voice, but it all belongs to Him. He is watching to see if you will steward that power wisely and use it to do His work. He is watching to see if you will use your influence and authority to share His love with a lost and dying world. That is the Power Test. Will you pass it?

For Further Reflection

Acts 1:8

Ephesians 3:20

1 Corinthians 6:14

Luke 24:49

2 Corinthians 12:9

Key Quotes

God created us to have power, and He wants to give His power to us, but He is looking for those who can be trusted with it.

The Power Test often comes suddenly.

Power isn't ours to own, and it can be taken away just as quickly as it is given. God wants us to recognize that all power comes from Him, and He wants us to walk in humility.

Power is given for the purpose of helping others.

He is watching to see if you will handle that power wisely and use it to do His work.

CHAPTER EIGHT

The Prosperity Test

As we discovered in the previous chapter, power will test your character. But so will money. In fact, money is really just another form of power. Money can give us the power to do certain things or meet certain needs, and in the same way, the lack of money can hinder us from doing certain things. Therefore, money empowers us to some extent. It also tests our character.

The Prosperity Test: Using Money Wisely

So we must ask ourselves, *What do we do with the power our money brings us?* Do we use it as God would have us use it—to further His purposes for our lives and the lives of others? Or do we squander it in foolish ways, or worse yet, in ways that are actually harmful? This is the Prosperity Test.

What are some of the basic material needs we have that require money to purchase?

_____

_____

_____

_____

What is the purpose of money, and how does God distribute it?

_____

_____

_____

_____

Describe the vision Pharaoh saw in Genesis 41:1–7. What was Pharaoh's reaction to the dreams (v. 8)?

_____

_____

_____

_____

Here is Joseph's interpretation to Pharaoh:

Then Joseph said to Pharaoh, "The dreams of Pharaoh are one; God has shown Pharaoh what He is about to do: The seven good cows are seven years, and the seven good heads are seven years; the dreams are one. And the seven thin and ugly cows which came up after them are seven years, and the seven empty heads blighted by the east wind are seven years of famine. This is the thing which I have spoken to Pharaoh. God has shown Pharaoh what He is about to do. Indeed seven years of great plenty will come throughout all the land of Egypt; but after them seven years of famine will arise, and all the plenty will be forgotten in the land of Egypt; and the famine will deplete the land. So the plenty will not be known in the land because of the famine following, for it will be very severe. And the dream was repeated to Pharaoh twice because the thing is established by God, and God will shortly bring it to pass." (Genesis 41:25–32)

What did Joseph tell Pharaoh was about to happen?

_____

_____

_____

_____

Summarize Joseph's practical recommendation to Pharaoh in verses 33–36.

_____

_____

_____

_____

What were the characteristics the leader needed to have?

_____

_____

_____

_____

The story continues:

So the advice was good in the eyes of Pharaoh and in the eyes of all his servants. And Pharaoh said to his servants, "Can we find such a one as this, a man in whom is the Spirit of God?"

Then Pharaoh said to Joseph, "Inasmuch as God has shown you all this, there is no one as discerning and wise as you. You shall be over my house, and all my people shall be ruled according to your word; only in regard to the throne will I be greater than you." And Pharaoh said to Joseph, "See, I have set you over all the land of Egypt." (vv. 37–41)

In verse 38, Pharaoh asks his servants who might be right for the job. In this verse, what is the one characteristic Pharaoh suggests is a requirement for the job?

_____

_____

_____

_____

Do we hear any response from Pharaoh's servants as to candidates before Pharaoh seeks out Joseph? What does this suggest about who was in control of the process?

_____

_____

_____

_____

Did Joseph suggest himself to handle this responsibility? According to verse 39, why did Pharaoh select Joseph to be his second in command?

_____

_____

_____

_____

God had a plan to provide food for everyone when the years of famine came. But His plan would have failed in the hands of someone who didn't know how to manage money wisely. God looked for someone who was a good steward, someone who knew how to manage material things according to His principles. The Prosperity Test was a huge part of Joseph's destiny. Would he manage the wealth of those years of plenty as God wanted?

The Prosperity Test is a huge part of your destiny as well. Until you are found faithful with money, you will not be able to step into your destiny to the full extent God desires. Why? Because God's plans for you will always involve bringing His blessings and provision to others.

Does passing the Prosperity Test depend upon the level of resources you have? Explain.

_____

_____

_____

_____

Agnes Gonxha Bojaxhiu, also known as Mother Teresa, learned about the principle of stewardship and generosity from her mother at an early age:

In 1919, when Mother Teresa—then Agnes—was only eight years old, her father suddenly fell ill and died. ... In the aftermath of her father's death, Agnes became extraordinarily close to her mother [Drana], a pious and compassionate woman who instilled in her daughter a deep commitment to charity. Although by no means wealthy, Drana Bojaxhiu extended an open invitation to the city's destitute to dine with her family. "My child, never eat a single mouthful unless you are sharing it with others," she counseled her daughter. When Agnes asked who the people eating with them were, her mother uniformly responded, "Some of them are our relations, but all of them are our people."[1]

Mother Teresa's family was not poor, as her father had a successful business before his death. But in 1928 she became a nun, first in Dublin, Ireland, and three years later in Darjeeling, India. She taught school to the poorest Bengali families. She took her final vow of poverty and obedience to her convent in 1937. In 1946, Mother Teresa received a second calling: a direct word from Christ to abandon teaching and work in the slums of Calcutta serving the poorest and sickest people.

Mother Teresa had to wait until January 1948 to get permission from the convent for her to leave teaching. She then left the convent in August of that year to go to the city.[2]

What do you think about what Mother Teresa's mother told her?

Mother Teresa was not supported by any large foundations or charities before she went out on her own to found Missionaries of Charity. When she passed away in 1997, Missionaries of Charity had more than 4,000 nuns—in addition to thousands more volunteers—with 610 orphanages, soup kitchens, homeless shelters, and clinics in 123 countries around the world.[3] She is considered one of the greatest humanitarians of the twentieth century, received the Nobel Peace Prize, and was canonized as a saint after her death. How does the story of Mother Teresa show how God can work when someone responds to His call, regardless of the resources they may have at the time?

_____

_____

_____

_____

Read Mark 12:41–44. How does this story relate to that of Mother Teresa?

_____

_____

_____

_____

You Take the Prosperity Test *Every* Day

The United States is one of the most prosperous nations in the world. What does the list of average annual household incomes in the text show about prosperity in the US versus other countries?

_____

_____

_____

_____

Many of us have absolutely no comprehension of how the rest of the world lives. Here in America, many people live in a prosperity bubble, and most have no idea how richly blessed and prosperous we are. We are living the Prosperity Test every day. Whether we realize it or not, we have been entrusted with great material wealth.

Although our nation is wealthy as a whole, that does not mean there is not a financial need in America to address. The national poverty rate in the US in 2021 was 12.8 percent; the child poverty rate was 16.8 percent.[4] The federal poverty income level (FPL) for a family of four that year was $26,500.[5] The average rent for a one-room apartment in a city like New York or San Francisco is over $3,000 a month—more than the FPL.

Read these verses and describe what our attitude should be toward the poor among us: Proverbs 19:17, 28:27; 1 John 3:17–18; Luke 12:33–36; Deuteronomy 15:10–11; Ezekiel 16:49.

_____

_____

_____

_____

The critical question is, *What are you going to do with your wealth?* In the same way power tests the true character of every person, money tests it, too. Every time you get your paycheck, you have a test handed to you.

According to the text, which type of income is particularly revealing? Why?

_____

_____

_____

_____

What lesson do Matthew 6:21 and 1 Samuel 16:7 teach about how the Lord judges His people?

_____

_____

_____

So it's very important to settle these questions: What has first place in your heart—God or money? Does money control you, or do you control money?

_____

_____

_____

_____

Let God Be First

The most important principle I can tell you about money can be summed up in four simple words: *Let God be first!*

I always feel burdened to share this principle with people because it's so important. I feel so passionate that I even wrote a whole book about it called *The Blessed Life*. When God is number one in your life, everything else adds up!

Read Proverbs 3:9. How do we honor the Lord?

_____

_____

_____

_____

Finances are just one way we can show honor to God and let Him know He is first in our lives. Joseph honored God and let Him be first in everything he had. Joseph even honored God in the naming of his children.

What two words show how Joseph remembered and honored God when he named his firstborn children?

_____

_____

What did he name his two children, and what did those names mean?

_____

_____

_____

_____

God has always been interested in knowing what is *first* place in our hearts.

How does the story of Cain and Abel (see Genesis 4:3–5) show this principle?

_____

_____

_____

_____

When the Israelites first entered the Promised Land, what did God command Israel do with the silver and gold from Jericho? How does this illustrate the principle of firstfruits?

_____

_____

_____

_____

What did Achan do with some of the silver, and what were the consequences?

_____

_____

_____

_____

The tithe is always the *first* part, not the last. God said that when the Israelites' sheep had lambs, they were to give the *first* lamb to Him. God did not say to let the sheep have ten lambs, and then give one of the ten to Him. He said to give Him the *first* one. Why? *Because it takes faith to give the first one!* It takes faith to give the *first* 10 percent, not the last 10 percent. Tithing means a tenth part, but it's about giving the *first* tenth to God!

What are we saying to God when we give Him the *last* 10 percent?

_____

_____

_____

_____

What are we saying to God when we give Him the *first* 10 percent?

_____

_____

_____

_____

Read Malachi 3:8–12. What does God say will happen if the people tithe?

_____

_____

_____

_____

What does God say will happen if the people do not tithe?

_____

_____

_____

_____

What does "And I will rebuke the devourer for your sakes" (v. 11) mean in your own words?

_____

_____

_____

_____

What would it mean to you to receive the blessings God offers in this passage?

_____

_____

_____

_____

Malachi 3:10 is unique in being the only place in the Bible where God says, "try Me" or "test Me." So if you're still not convinced, try tithing for a year and see what happens. I've told our congregation that if they're not fully satisfied, we'll give them their money back. It's a money-back guarantee!

Do you tithe to your home church? Why or why not?

_____

_____

_____

_____

If you decided to try tithing, what criteria would you use when the year was up to determine whether you were "satisfied"?

_____

_____

_____

_____

According to the Barna data cited about donation trends, what is happening to church tithing and giving?

_____

_____

_____

_____

I believe God has blessed this nation because we have sent missionaries all around the world to spread His gospel message. America has been living in years of prosperity and blessings from God. But I also believe that years of famine are right around the corner if we do not start honoring Him with the firstfruits of those blessings.

Any time you receive your paycheck or some unexpected money, you have a great opportunity to let God be first. When you get a bonus, do you tithe on it? Do you honor God first? Imagine the message it sends when someone prays, "God, please help me! I need extra money!" But when God answers that prayer by sending the extra money, they don't tithe on it!

Isn't it amazing how quickly we forget it was God who met our need and sent us the money? Tithing is simply a way of expressing our gratitude to God and acknowledging that it came from Him. But if we immediately forget God and don't honor Him with the tithe on that money, we are not putting Him first.

Please understand me. This is not law—this is *love*. This is expressing love and gratitude and honor to God, the One who has given us everything!

Have you ever received an unexpected blessing after a decision to tithe or give generously? Explain.

_____

_____

_____

_____

Tithing isn't only about making sure you're not under a curse or about moving forward in your destiny. It's also about gratitude and showing God that He has the first place in your heart.

So let God be first—this is the first principle of the Prosperity Test. Joseph understood this principle and put God first in every area of his life.

There are other important financial principles that were essential to his success in his destiny as ruler of the world's food supply during the years of famine. Joseph understood the most *important* principle—he allowed God to be first in every area of his life. But Joseph also understood the importance of something else we would all do well to comprehend: *learning to wait.*

Good Things Come

For those seven years of abundance, Joseph made the Egyptians store up, store up, and store up some more.

What virtue, mentioned in the Prison Test chapter, does Joseph force the people to exercise during this period of waiting (see also James 1:2–4)? Why is that important?

_____

_____

_____

Why do get-rich-quick schemes have no place in the life of a believer?

_____

_____

_____

In your own words, what is the reason for most people's desire for instant gratification?

_____

_____

_____

Are you prone to making impulse purchases? Have you ever regretted an impulse purchase? Explain.

_____

_____

_____

What should we do instead of making an impulse purchase—or any impulse decision, for that matter?

_____

_____

_____

Can You Afford It?

Thankfully, there's a simple way to prevent conflict and pressure from dominating your financial decisions: a budget.

What was Joseph's "budget" plan for the storing up of grain in Egypt (see Genesis 41:34–35)?

_____

_____

_____

In verse 35, under whose authority was the storing of grain ordered? How did that make the people and the officers of Egypt accountable?

_____

_____

_____

_____

Describe the process and purpose of having specific limits and accountability using "Mr. Budget." Why does it help to use the "Mr. Budget" phrasing?

_____

_____

_____

_____

How should you approach whether you can afford something?

_____

_____

_____

_____

Budgeting is also about being aligned with the Lord and stewarding your resources well. You might get to a place where you can buy just about anything you want. You could be blessed financially, but that doesn't mean you *should* buy anything you want. The question, "God, is this Your will?" is always important.

What do you think about a multi-billionaire buying a $1.5 billion yacht? (That is not a typo.) In your opinion, could such a purchase ever be morally justified? Why or why not?

_____

_____

_____

_____

Change Your Life—Make a Budget!

What are the seven reasons to make a budget and how might they change your life? Briefly respond to each.

- _____

  _____

  _____

  _____

- _____

  _____

  _____

  _____

- _____

  _____

_____

_____

- _____

_____

_____

_____

- _____

_____

_____

_____

- _____

_____

_____

_____

- _____

_____

_____

_____

As with everything else God has given you stewardship over, He is watching to see if you will handle money wisely. Having a budget is a first step toward taking responsibility for your money and showing God you will be faithful with the things He has placed in your care.

Live Below Your Means

Joseph developed his budget so well that after seven years of savings, he fed the entire world during seven years of famine. One way Joseph did it was by living on less than the amount that was actually coming in—this is called "living below your means."

How should we calculate and allocate our income to live below our means?

_____

_____

_____

_____

How did living in a trailer for several years after Debbie and I first got married contribute to financial freedom?

_____

_____

_____

_____

Have you or do you need to make a similar kind of choice for a few years to gain financial freedom?

_____

_____

_____

_____

Are you influenced by what other people have? Can you recall a specific instance? Explain.

_____

_____

_____

_____

With what does 1 Timothy 6:6–10 say we should be content?

_____

_____

_____

_____

Verse 10 is often misquoted. What does it actually say is the root of all kinds of evil?

_____

_____

What does this passage say happens to "those who desire to be rich" and "have strayed from their faith in their greediness"?

_____

_____

_____

_____

How is this same truth expressed in Ecclesiastes 5:10?

_____

_____

_____

Can you think of some examples from personal experience or from public figures that demonstrate this principle?

_____

_____

_____

_____

Which of these examples of greed are you familiar with? A Ponzi scheme (named after Charles Ponzi in the 1920s)? Bernie Madoff? Perhaps the Enron scandal? In 2022, the leader of a bitcoin trading company was indicted for an alleged theft of perhaps $10 billion. What do all of these examples have in common with the characters in the following story? How does it show the same principle?

> But a certain man named Ananias, with Sapphira his wife, sold a posses-
> sion. And he kept back part of the proceeds, his wife also being aware
> of it, and brought a certain part and laid it at the apostles' feet. But
> Peter said, "Ananias, why has Satan filled your heart to lie to the Holy
> Spirit and keep back part of the price of the land for yourself? While
> it remained, was it not your own? And after it was sold, was it not in
> your own control? Why have you conceived this thing in your heart?
> You have not lied to men but to God."
>
> Then Ananias, hearing these words, fell down and breathed his last.
> So great fear came upon all those who heard these things. And the
> young men arose and wrapped him up, carried him out, and buried
> him.
>
> Now it was about three hours later when his wife came in, not
> knowing what had happened. And Peter answered her, "Tell me whether
> you sold the land for so much?"
>
> She said, "Yes, for so much."

Then Peter said to her, "How is it that you have agreed together to test the Spirit of the Lord? Look, the feet of those who have buried your husband are at the door, and they will carry you out." Then immediately she fell down at his feet and breathed her last. And the young men came in and found her dead, and carrying her out, buried her by her husband. So great fear came upon all the church and upon all who heard these things. (Acts 5:1–11)

_____

_____

_____

_____

What declaration do you make to God when you live above your means?

_____

_____

_____

_____

Make no mistake about it: God *wants* to give us more. He wants to bless us and give us the desires of our hearts. But it's so we can bless others! And as with everything else, in order to have God's blessings, we must do things His way and abide by His principles. And once people become better stewards and get their finances in order, they're more likely to break free from bad financial habits and debt patterns. Understanding these biblical principles changes everything!

People who don't follow God's financial principles often blame God for not coming through, but their financial problems are their own fault, not God's. They have fallen prey to the *deceitfulness* of riches.

Don't Be Deceived

Yes, riches can be deceitful. In 1 Timothy 6:9–10, the apostle Paul tells us that riches can cause people to fall into a snare and stray from the faith. Jesus put it this way:

> Now these are the ones sown among thorns; they are the ones who hear the word, and the cares of this world, the deceitfulness of riches, and the desires for other things entering in choke the word, and it becomes unfruitful. (Mark 4:18–19)

What does it mean to "choke the word [of God]"? How does this relate to the parable of the soils in Luke 8:12–15 we mentioned earlier? Explain.

_____

_____

_____

_____

What has been an extreme result of deceitfulness of riches for some people?

_____

_____

_____

_____

What would you say to someone who believed that attending church and giving would help them get rich?

_____

_____

_____

I gave the example of spending ten dollars a day on coffee as possibly being extravagant. It may seem extreme, but ten dollars is more than a person working at the federal minimum wage earns in an hour of work. What principle does this kind of spending demonstrate?

_____

_____

_____

_____

Prayerfully and carefully evaluate your own financial situation (and that of your family, if appropriate). What areas of your finances could and should you address and improve?

_____

_____

_____

_____

How will you address those areas?

_____

_____

_____

_____

What areas of your attitude and behavior should you address regarding finances and your heart?

_____

_____

_____

_____

How will you address those areas?

_____

_____

_____

_____

God never intended for us to miss out on realizing our God-given dreams, and God will give us everything we need to fulfill the destiny to which He has called us. The question is, *What will we do with the things He has given us?*

Let God be first in your finances. Honor Him with the firstfruits of all your increase. Make a budget, live below your means, and learn to wait for the good things God has promised. When you have been found faithful in handling money, you will pass the Prosperity Test. Then God will be able to promote you, just as He did Joseph, and use you as a channel to distribute His wealth and resources to a hurting and destitute world.

For Further Reflection

Philippians 4:19

2 Corinthians 9:8

Proverbs 10:22

Psalm 84:11

1 Corinthians 4:2

Luke 16:1–13

Key Quotes

Money is really just another form of power.

God's plans for you will always involve bringing His blessings and provision to others.

Here in America, many people live in a prosperity bubble, and most of us have no idea how richly blessed and prosperous we are.

The most important principle I can tell you about money can be summed up in four simple words: Let God be first! ... When God is number one in your life, everything else adds up!

Let God be first in your finances. Honor Him with the firstfruits of all your increase. Make a budget, live below your means, and learn to wait for the good things God has promised.

CHAPTER NINE

The Pardon Test

What was going through young Joseph's mind as he made that long and painful journey to Egypt? As he stood on an auction block and was sold to the highest bidder? As he served in the house of Potiphar as a slave? As he became a husband and a father but could not share his joy with his father, all because of his brothers' sin and hatred?

What is your immediate reaction or response to these questions?

_____

_____

_____

_____

The Pardon Test: Forgiving Wrongs

Joseph had valid reasons to feel betrayed and abused. The suffering Joseph endured came about because of the deliberate cruelty and malice of others, so Joseph most certainly had reason to be hurt, angry, and hungry for justice.

What passage of Scripture shows us Joseph decided to forgive? Explain.

_____

_____

_____

_____

This is the Pardon Test, and every one of us must face this test and pass it. Like Joseph, every one of us will have to deal with hurtful relationships and wrong or even malicious behavior. It can be easy to forgive when the offense is something minor, but what about when it's major? Like being sold into slavery by your brothers?

Should your response or reaction to an offense be based on the level or seriousness of the offense? Why or why not?

_____

_____

_____

_____

Joseph passed the Pardon Test with flying colors. Let's look ahead at the moment when Joseph shares his forgiveness:

When Joseph's brothers saw that their father was dead, they said, "Perhaps Joseph will hate us, and may actually repay us for all the evil which we did to him." So they sent messengers to Joseph, saying, "Before your father died he commanded, saying, 'Thus you shall say to Joseph: "I beg you, please forgive the trespass of your brothers and their sin; for they did evil to you.'" Now, please, forgive the trespass of the servants of the God of your father." And Joseph wept when they spoke to him.

Then his brothers also went and fell down before his face, and they said, "Behold, we are your servants."

Joseph said to them, "Do not be afraid, for am I in the place of God? But as for you, you meant evil against me; but God meant it for good, in order to bring it about as it is this day, to save many people alive. Now therefore, do not be afraid; I will provide for you and your little ones." And he comforted them and spoke kindly to them. (Genesis 50:15–21)

This passage is the very first time the word "forgive" is used in the Bible. Does this surprise you, considering the offenses of God's children He had dealt with in the past? Explain.

_____

_____

_____

_____

What is the meaning of the Hebrew word for "forgive"?

_____

_____

_____

_____

How is the word more often translated (about 208 times as compared to 102 times in the New King James Version)?

_____

_____

_____

_____

Read Isaiah 53:6–12. How does this passage demonstrate true forgiveness?

_____

_____

_____

_____

The message Joseph's brothers claimed to be bringing from their father asked Joseph to *lift off* the sin they had done against him. Their message asked Joseph to forgive them completely—to absolve them of guilt and pardon them.

What happens when the president or a governor pardons someone in the US justice system?

_____

_____

_____

A popular analogy compares holding unforgiveness in your heart to drinking poison and hoping it will hurt the other person. But the reality is that *you* are the only one who will get hurt! Unforgiveness causes you to live in torment.

Jesus describes this for us in Matthew 18, where He tells the story of the servant who refused to forgive his fellow servant. This is one of the most profound teachings on forgiveness in the Bible. Jesus says the master of the unforgiving servant "delivered him to the torturers until he should pay all that was due" (Matthew 18:34).

What point is Jesus making in verse 34?

_____

_____

_____

_____

Read all of Matthew 18.

What did the disciples want to know in verse 1?

_____

_____

_____

_____

What did that question show about their character? What did they lack according to verses 3–4?

_____

_____

_____

_____

Some of this passage talks about sins against "little ones" or "little children." Consider verse 5. Do you think Jesus is only talking about sins against children (as in age) in verses 6–14? Explain.

_____

_____

_____

_____

How often should we forgive a brother who sins against us (see Matthew 18:22)? What do you think is the meaning of this number?

_____

_____

_____

_____

Have you or someone you know ever been in a situation like that of the forgiving master or unforgiving servant? What happened?

_____

_____

_____

_____

When we hold unforgiveness in our hearts, it hurts us. But it also hinders us from moving forward into our destiny. If we want to step into the things God has planned for our lives, what must we learn to do?

_____

_____

_____

_____

Keys to Forgiveness: Release, Receive, and Believe

I believe the Holy Spirit has shown me some keys about walking in God's forgiveness. To forgive as God has forgiven us, we must learn to release, receive, and believe.

Release

According to the text, what does it mean to forgive others completely?

_____

_____

_____

_____

What would it look like to "forgive" someone partially?

_____

_____

_____

_____

How did God choose to forgive and release us?

_____

_____

_____

Have you ever thought about why God chose that method? Why didn't He just wave His hand and declare us clean?

_____

_____

_____

_____

Joseph made the choice to *release* his brothers and forgive them completely for everything they had done to him. He had to choose to go on with God or be consumed with bitterness for the rest of his life.

Joseph chose to move forward with the blessing of God, and I believe he did this long before he had this conversation with his brothers.

How old was Joseph when he met his brothers in Genesis 50? What is the reasoning for believing that Joseph had already released them from their offense against him?

_____

_____

_____

_____

"Before your father died he commanded, saying, 'Thus you shall say to Joseph: "I beg you, please forgive the trespass of your brothers and their sin; for they did evil to you."' Now, please, forgive the trespass of the servants of the God of your father." And Joseph wept when they spoke to him. (Genesis 50:16–17)

Describe how this was manipulative. What parts of it stand out? Do you think there was any hint of apology or repentance in the brothers' words or actions?

_____

_____

_____

_____

Is it difficult for you to forgive someone who does not admit their sin? Why is it so much harder to forgive someone who does not admit their sin?

_____

_____

_____

_____

That is the true test of forgiveness and the essence of the Pardon Test. We must forgive, even if those who have wronged us never realize what they have done or repent of it. We must *release* them and leave the situation in God's hands.

How does Joseph's response in Genesis 50:19 show the truth about who is just (the Judge) and how we are justified?

_____

_____

_____

_____

Any time you hold unforgiveness against someone, you have set yourself up as judge and jury. You have made yourself the one who determines that person's guilt or punishment. When you do this, what are you saying to God?

_____

_____

_____

_____

But when you forgive someone, you release God to act in the situation, in your life, and in that other person's life. You let Him be the Judge He rightfully is. We are all ultimately accountable to Him.

Describe a season or event in your life when you had a hard time forgiving. What was the result?

_____

_____

_____

_____

Is there a wound or offense you're holding onto today that needs to be addressed? If so, what will you do to address it?

_____

_____

_____

I share the story of a time when I had not truly released someone from their offense against me. I even argued with God about it.

Is there anyone you have not truly released even though you may think you have? Explain.

_____

_____

_____

_____

I eventually released that person from their offense. (God won the argument—funny how He always does!) Then I prayed for him.

What would you pray for someone you had forgiven?

_____

_____

_____

_____

Once you have forgiven someone, what opposition might you expect? What form might it take?

_____

_____

_____

_____

What do you think about what James Robison wrote in my Bible: "I have nothing to prove. I have Someone to please"? What does it mean to you?

_____

_____

_____

_____

Read Leviticus 19:18 and Romans 12:19–21. What do these passages tell us about vengeance?

_____

_____

_____

_____

Receive

The Bible makes it very clear there is a connection between our forgiveness of others and God's forgiveness of us. I suppose you have prayed the Lord's Prayer at one time or another. Jesus taught us to pray this way:

And forgive us our debts,
As we forgive our debtors.
And do not lead us into temptation,
But deliver us from the evil one.
For Yours is the kingdom and the power and the glory forever. Amen.
(Matthew 6:12–13)

How does this passage relate forgiveness and temptation?

_____

_____

_____

_____

How should we forgive the sins of others?

_____

_____

_____

_____

Jesus continues:

For if you forgive men their trespasses, your heavenly Father will also forgive you. But if you do not forgive men their trespasses, neither will your Father forgive your trespasses. (vv. 14–15)

What happens if we don't forgive the sins of others? Do you consider these verses a promise or a warning? Explain.

_____

_____

_____

_____

How does this passage relate to our freedom in Christ? What happens if we don't forgive?

_____

_____

_____

_____

Why is it difficult to give forgiveness if we have never received (accepted or acknowledged) it?

_____

_____

_____

_____

If you believe you must somehow *earn* your forgiveness, you will make other people earn their forgiveness, too. If you believe that somehow you are *paying* for your forgiveness, you will make others pay for forgiveness also.

We fall into this trap all too often. Sometimes we live as though God Himself is keeping score, even though He gave us the best gift He had—His beloved Son—to set us free from the penalty of our sins! We pray as if God is getting back at us for all the stuff we've done wrong. We look at misfortunes in life as God's way of getting even.

How might we try to "keep score" with God?

_____

_____

_____

_____

Have you ever "kept score" with God? Explain.

_____

_____

_____

_____

Remember: *God will never get back at you.* He is never going to get even with you or punish you or make you pay for the wrongs you have done. Why? Because Jesus already paid your penalty in full! Isaiah 53:10 says, "It pleased the LORD to bruise Him." How could it have pleased God to bruise His own Son? It pleased Him because all our sin was atoned for, and He could once again have a relationship with us. That is the goodness of God. That is the forgiveness of God. But for some of us, it just seems too good to be true. We have to learn to *receive* it.

How was my behavior toward Debbie counterproductive in the story about me stepping on her toe? What was the cause of my "hit me" mentality? Have you ever experienced this?

_____

_____

_____

_____

God disciplines His children. That word in Hebrew does not mean to punish. Look up the root of the word "discipline." What does it mean?

_____

_____

_____

_____

We may deserve punishment, but instead God forgives us and does not punish us. What is the word for that character trait of God?

_____

_____

_____

_____

Matthew 23:23 says, "Woe to you, scribes and Pharisees, hypocrites! For you pay tithe of mint and anise and cummin, and have neglected the weightier matters of the law: justice and mercy and faith."

We leave *justice* to God and thank Him for His *mercy*—that we don't receive what we deserve.

But if you have a problem *receiving* God's forgiveness, it could be because you have a problem *believing* it.

Believe

According to Scripture, God cannot even look on our sin, but His eyes are on the righteous every day. God is pure, just, and holy, and we have fallen far short of His perfection. So how did God create a relationship with us so He could accept us and look at us (see 2 Corinthians 5:21 and Romans 6:14)?

_____

_____

_____

_____

Explain why people don't go to hell for their sin, but rather for unbelief. How did the great exchange work?

_____

_____

_____

_____

What is the miracle explained in Psalm 103:12?

_____

_____

_____

_____

I can have a relationship with God, and it's not because I did something good or somehow earned it. The only reason I can have a relationship with God and stand before Him without guilt, sin, or shame is because God laid all my iniquity on His Son, Jesus Christ. When God looks at me now, He sees me washed in the blood of Jesus, and that blood makes me pure and holy in His sight.

Read Hebrews 9:22 and Leviticus 17:11. What is the role of blood in atonement?

_____

_____

_____

_____

This is what you must believe: You *are* righteous! His eyes *are* upon you! God has *removed your sin*. You can have a relationship with Him now. He wants to walk with you, speak to you, and show you great things every day.

How does this truth make you feel?

_____

_____

_____

_____

What are we able to do now that we have been pardoned and forgiven?

_____

_____

_____

_____

Think of all the wrong you have ever done—God has forgiven it all! You have been forgiven. Now you need to share that forgiveness!

Explain in your own words how the grandson of Holocaust victims and the grandson of a Nazi prison guard could possibly reconcile as Marty Waldman and his friend did.

_____

_____

_____

_____

You might also be encouraged by the story of Corrie ten Boom and her encounter with a former Nazi prison guard who was responsible for the death of her sister.[1]

When you hold on to unforgiveness, you are only hurting yourself. But when you forgive, you will be gloriously free! You will be free of torment, free of judgment, and free to move forward into the destiny God has planned for your life.

For Further Reflection

1 John 1:9

Isaiah 55:7

Mark 11:25

Ephesians 4:32

Leviticus 19:18

Key Quotes

Every one of us will have to deal with hurtful relationships and wrong or even malicious behavior. It can be easy to forgive when the offense is something minor, but what about when it's major?

That is the true test of forgiveness and the essence of the Pardon Test.... We must release them and leave the situation in God's hands.

God will never get back at you. He is never going to get even with you or punish you or make you pay for the wrongs you have done.

This is what you must believe: You are righteous! His eyes are upon you! God has removed your sin. You can have a relationship with Him now.

When you forgive, you will be gloriously free!

CHAPTER TEN

The Purpose Test

Twenty-two years had passed since Joseph was sold into Egypt. He had spent thirteen years working as a slave, and part of that time included being imprisoned in a dungeon as punishment for a crime he did not commit.

Suddenly, after more than two decades, his brothers—the very ones who had betrayed him and caused him so much suffering—were bowing down before him just as his dreams had symbolically depicted so many years before! The Bible tells us what Joseph was thinking at that moment: "Then Joseph remembered the dreams which he had dreamed about them" (Genesis 42:9).

Have you ever had a sudden revelation about an important event or part of your life? What was it and how did you feel? Explain.

_____

_____

What other feelings or reactions could Joseph have had? Do you think he might have had mixed feelings? Explain.

_____

_____

_____

_____

The Purpose Test:
Understanding Your Destiny

When you read Genesis 45:3–8, you see that Joseph finally understood his purpose. He not only understood the dreams God had given him but also the *purpose* those dreams had foreshadowed. Joseph realized he had finally stepped into the destiny for which God had created him.

Summarize in your own words Joseph's response in Genesis 45:8–13.

_____

_____

_____

_____

Believe You Have a Purpose

What must you know and understand in order to discover God's unique purpose for your life?

_____

_____

_____

_____

God has an eternal purpose for everything, and the body of Christ has an overall purpose in God's eternal plan. But it's important to know that you, as an individual, have a *specific purpose* as well.

In addition to having our own specific purposes, how might we as believers describe our part of the broader purpose within the body of Christ?

_____

_____

_____

_____

According to Psalm 139, when was your purpose determined by God?

_____

_____

_____

_____

According to the book, what does God want you to discover about that purpose? What will happen when you do?

_____

_____

_____

_____

_____

_____

_____

_____

How did God inspire me to use my gift and passion to preach when I was working in the church nursery? What tasks or jobs can you approach with this same mindset?

_____

_____

_____

_____

When God created you, He had a specific purpose in mind, and He has given you a specific gifting related to your purpose. You need to discover what your gifting is, because when you discover the gifting God created in you, it will bring energy and excitement to your life. More importantly, it will help other people. And as you move in your gifting, you will understand your purpose.

What is the first step to determining what your specific purpose might be?

_____

_____

_____

_____

God has a unique purpose for your life, and it's vitally important for you to believe it—to *believe* He created you with a specific purpose in mind. I encourage you to make every effort to discover what your purpose is. As you move toward discovering His purpose for your life, you will also be moving toward your destiny.

What is the difference between "purpose" and "destiny"? Explain.

_____

_____

_____

_____

Understand God Is in Control

Consider the story of the pessimistic parachutist. Are you, or have you ever been, someone who expects the worst to happen? If so, describe a specific circumstance.

_____

_____

_____

_____

Would your spouse, children, or friends say you are an optimist or pessimist?

_____

_____

_____

_____

What factors might lead someone to have or develop a pessimistic attitude? Explain.

_____

_____

_____

_____

You must know that God is in control. If you don't believe God is in control, you will live in a sad, anxious, and bewildering world—a world with little purpose. When you can't see the hand of God working, you will eventually reach a point where you only see the bad in everything and always expect the worst to happen.

According to the text, what will happen when you truly believe that God is in control?

_____

_____

_____

_____

What was Joseph's attitude about what had happened in his life? In your own words, what had he learned and how was that attitude expressed in Genesis 45:5, 7–8?

_____

_____

_____

_____

We, too, must come to trust God as Joseph did. We need to stop thinking we will not fulfill our destiny because of something someone else did.

Whether it was your parents or an abusive pastor or a boss who wronged you—no one can stop God's destiny for you! We must understand that God can take even the wrongs done to us and use them for our good.

How can God take our mistakes and failures and use them for our own good?

_____

_____

_____

_____

What is the important truth in Isaiah 55:9 we often overlook?

_____

_____

_____

My son Josh learned a lesson years ago when living in an apartment in Amarillo, Texas. What was the truth he learned? Can you share an example of this truth from your own life or the life of someone you know?

_____

_____

_____

_____

How should you act—and what should you believe—when you have prayerfully made a decision and are not sure whether it was the right one or the best one?

_____

_____

_____

_____

Is the devil in control? Explain.

_____

_____

_____

_____

Read Hebrews 2:14–15, 2 Thessalonians 2:8, and Ephesians 6:10–12. What do these verses teach about the "power" of Satan?

_____

_____

_____

_____

Read Matthew 17:14–21. Jesus had just come down from the Mount of Transfiguration with the disciples. Why had the disciples not been able to cast out this demon? What would be required (v. 21)?

_____

_____

_____

_____

What lesson do you take from this passage?

_____

_____

_____

_____

Read Luke 4:1–14. What had Jesus received after His water baptism (v. 1)? What was the source of His power (v. 14)?

_____

_____

_____

_____

What does it mean if Jesus resisted all Satan's temptations and we possess the same Spirit as Jesus?

_____

_____

_____

_____

Explain how Romans 8:28 and Isaiah 55:10–11 assure us that God's purpose will always be achieved. How does He make this happen?

_____

_____

_____

_____

How would you explain to someone going through a difficult time how God is in control?

_____

_____

_____

_____

Discover Your Gift

An important key to understanding your purpose is discovering the gifts God has given you. Why would God call you to do something and not give you the gifts to do it? He has designed you with a purpose in mind, so the gifts He has given you will always be related to your purpose in some significant way. If you look at the gifts God has given you, they will tell you a lot about your purpose. Your gifts can help you understand your God-given destiny.

Respond to these questions: What has God gifted me to do? What am I good at doing? What excites me? What brings me joy? What makes me feel alive?

_____

_____

_____

_____

_____

_____

_____

_____

_____

_____

_____

_____

Why are we sometimes reluctant to accept the idea that God wants us to enjoy life and give us good things? Have you ever felt that way? Explain.

_____

_____

_____

_____

Describe the three types of gifts God gives His people.

_____

_____

_____

_____

_____

_____

_____

_____

_____

According to Romans 12:6, how are we expected to use our gifts? Explain.

_____

_____

_____

In your own words, how does Romans 12:4–8 explain the functions within the body of Christ?

_____

_____

_____

_____

What are the seven motivational gifts? Describe each in a sentence
or two.

- _____

_____

_____

_____

- _____

_____

_____

_____

- _____

_____

_____

_____

- _____

_____

_____

_____

- _____

_____

_____

_____

- _____
  _____
  _____
  _____

- _____
  _____
  _____
  _____

What gift do you think you have? Where would you likely fit in the "committee" example in the book?

_____
_____
_____
_____

There are many ways to determine your gifts, like spiritual gifts tests[1] or certain personality assessments. Have you ever completed a gifts or personality assessment? What were your results?

_____
_____
_____
_____

Your Purpose Gives Direction, Not Specifics

You may not have a specific picture of your complete destiny, but you do have a gift. And when you determine your gift, that will help bring *direction* to your life. Your purpose provides *direction* toward your destiny, but it's important to understand that your purpose does not contain the *specifics* of your destiny.

When will you know the specifics of your destiny?

_____

_____

_____

_____

It's important to understand this truth if you want to pass the Purpose Test: your gift and purpose will only point you toward your destiny, but they will not provide the *specifics*.

Explain how the gift of administration and its specifics were worked out in Joseph's life.

_____

_____

_____

What do we need to keep walking toward our destiny? Why does God wait to show us the specifics?

_____

_____

_____

_____

How does Psalm 119:105 describe how we are guided toward our destiny?

_____

_____

_____

How did the example of Abraham Lincoln demonstrate this truth?

_____

_____

_____

_____

Set Your Course and Be Faithful

We can all learn a lesson from Abraham Lincoln's example. Determine what your gift is and let it give you direction. Then *set your course* in that direction and simply *be faithful*. Don't get sidetracked trying to figure out the specifics. You get into trouble when you try to dictate the specifics to God.

Do you get sidetracked easily or try to dictate the specifics of your destiny to God? What happens when we try to imagine the specifics and things don't work out?

_____

_____

_____

_____

The Lord created every one of us with a purpose, but it's up to us to determine what we will do with that purpose.

The Lord sets a direction in front of each one of us, but our faithfulness determines how far we will go.

I was born with a gift to speak and teach, but I believe the number of people I can reach and help is determined by how many tests I pass and how faithful I stay to the Lord.

There are many tests you must go through on the way to your destiny, and all of these tests are important. Humility, character, stewardship, integrity, perseverance—all are important to fulfilling your destiny. But they can all be summed up in one word: faithfulness.

From the excerpts in his diary, how did John Wesley set his course and remain faithful to it?

_____

_____

_____

_____

More than anything else, faithfulness kept Joseph true on the path to God's destiny for him—saving millions of people. Faithfulness must also be the foundation for *our* lives. We must be faithful to God through all these tests. As we travel the road to our destiny, faithfulness is the anchor that will hold us steady through every storm. And faithfulness will keep us going until we pass every test and step into the fulfillment of our destinies in God.

Will you commit to be faithful to the Holy Spirit as He leads you through the storms of life toward your destiny? Explain.

_____

_____

_____

_____

For Further Reflection

Romans 8:28

Proverbs 19:21

2 Timothy 1:9

Proverbs 20:5

Colossians 3:23

Key Quotes

God has an eternal purpose for everything, and the body of Christ has an overall purpose in God's eternal plan. But it's important to know that you, as an individual, have a specific purpose as well.

When you discover the gifting God created in you, it will bring energy and excitement to your life. More importantly, it will help other people.

No one can stop God's destiny for you! We must understand that God can take even the wrongs done to us and use them for our good.

Your purpose provides direction toward your destiny, but ... your purpose does not contain the specifics of your destiny.

As we travel the road to our destiny, faithfulness is the anchor that will hold us steady through every storm.

Stay the Course

Chances are, as you read this, you're in one of two places. Maybe you're in a wilderness land somewhere between your dream and your destiny. Or maybe you're already walking in your destiny. No matter where you are, there are more tests ahead for you to face and pass.

You see, some of the tests we've examined in this book occurred in Joseph's life after his dream but before his destiny. Others occurred after he had already stepped into his destiny. But in order to fulfill his destiny to the fullest, he had to *continue* passing these tests. And the same is true for you.

What does 1 Corinthians 10:13 say about how God will test us? What word does God use for "test" in this verse?

_____

_____

_____

By whose power will we pass these character tests?

_____

_____

_____

_____

You may be in the midst of a real challenge right now. Be encouraged! You're that much closer to your destiny.

Your Destiny Is a Journey

I truly believe I am walking in the destiny God has for my life right now. There is incredible satisfaction in being where I am, and I feel extremely blessed. Yet it's also hard work. That's why we all go through these tests—so we are prepared for the blessings *and* the work that comes with fulfilling our destiny.

Your destiny is a journey. You may have heard the saying from Ralph Waldo Emerson: "It's not the destination, it's the journey." Or from T. S. Eliot: "The journey, not the destination, matters." Is that true for the believer?

On the one hand, for the believer the destination—*heaven*—matters. In fact, believers can expect to receive five crowns. Read 1 Corinthians 9:24–25; 1 Thessalonians 2:19; 2 Timothy 4:8; 1 Peter 5:4; Revelation 2:10. What are the five crowns? Describe them and what they mean in your own words.

_____

_____

_____

_____

_____

_____

_____

_____

_____

_____

On the other hand, if you are a believer, *how* you pursue your destiny is important; your character, which is shown by your works, matters. Though we are not saved by works, what we do matters. What does Ecclesiastes 12:14 say about what we do?

_____

_____

_____

_____

What does 2 Corinthians 5:10 say about our deeds?

_____

_____

_____

_____

What does James 2:14–26 say about our works? What is your response to the strong language James uses in this passage?

_____

_____

_____

_____

How are the destination and the journey intertwined?

_____

_____

_____

_____

God's destiny for us is much bigger than anything we can imagine. The more we seek to know Him, the more this realization will sink into our hearts and minds.

Like a pilot must continually hone their flying skills and competency, we must always *continue* to relearn and apply basic principles and not grow weary (see Galatians 6:9). According to the text, what are the six foundational activities of a healthy, faithful believer (note the Scripture passages)?

- _____

_____

_____

_____

- _____

_____

_____

_____

- _____

_____

_____

_____

- _____

_____

_____

_____

- _____

_____

_____

_____

- _____

_____

_____

_____

The ten character tests Joseph faced will help you develop the strong character necessary to support your God-given destiny. That's why it's so important to allow God to work in these areas of your life and to allow Him to develop patience, purity, perseverance, and true prosperity. Allow God to remove pride and the wrong motives for wanting power. Allow your heavenly Father to give you the grace to pardon those who have wronged you. Allow Him to reveal to you the glorious purpose for which He created you.

God's Purpose for You Is Extraordinary

Remember, the dreams God gives you are tailor-made for you. Like Joseph's dreams, they might not make sense right away or feel very significant. But trust that God is leading you toward an incredible and unique destiny.

Consider some of the individual stories in the book and study guide. Which of these resonated with you the most, and why? Write down some reactions or responses to those stories.

Isn't God amazing? His purpose for each one of us is extraordinary!

The journey may not look the way you expected, and it may be long and filled with trials, but do not lose heart! God gave you the dream, and He is preparing you for your destiny. May you continue to let God strengthen and deepen your character. May your God-given dream become your God-fulfilled destiny!

How did you view your destiny and the journey before reading this book?

_____

_____

_____

_____

_____

_____

_____

How do you view your destiny and the journey after reading this book?

_____

_____

_____

_____

_____

_____

_____

How will you commit to follow the example of Joseph—and the example of Christ—to fulfill your destiny?

_____

_____

_____

_____

_____

_____

_____

End Notes

Introduction

1   *Encyclopedia Brittanica Online*, s.v. "Andrew Lloyd Webber." Accessed February 7, 2023. https://www.britannica.com/biography/Andrew-Lloyd-Webber -Baron-Lloyd-Webber-of-Sydmonton#ref143133.

Chapter Four

1   "Women's Health Policy," Kaiser Family Foundation, accessed January 26, 2023, https://www.kff.org/womens-health-policy/fact-sheet/oral-contraceptive -pills/.

Chapter Six

1   One such reference tool is https://www.biblestudytools.com/interlinear -bible/.

2   *Fresh Start Bible* (Southlake, TX: Gateway Press, 2019).

Chapter Eight

1   "Mother Teresa Biography," *Biography*, updated February 24, 2020, https://www.biography.com/religious-figure/mother-teresa.

2   "Mother Teresa Biography."

3   "Mother Teresa Biography."

4   Craig Benson, "Poverty Rate of Children Higher Than National Rate, Lower for Older Populations," United States Census Bureau, October 4, 2022, https://www.census.gov/library/stories/2022/10/poverty-rate-varies-by-age-groups.html.

5   "Federal Poverty Level," Healthcare.gov, accessed January 31, 2023, https://www.healthcare.gov/glossary/federal-poverty-level-fpl.

Chapter Nine

1   See "I forgave the man who was co-responsible for my sister's death," Jesus.net, https://jesus.net/corrie-ten-boom-forgiveness/.

Chapter Ten

1   "Spiritual Gifts," Gateway Church, https://gatewaypeople.com/spiritual-gifts-assessment/study.